W9-BKY-823

The Oral History Manual

AMERICAN ASSOCIATION FOR STATE AND LOCAL HISTORY BOOK SERIES

PUBLICATIONS CHAIR

Ruby Rogers
Cincinnati Museum Center

EDITORIAL ADVISORY BOARD

J. D. Britton, Ohio Historical Society
David Donath, Woodstock Foundation, Inc.
D. Stephen Elliott, Council for America's First Freedom
Max J. Evans, Utah State Historical Society
Michael Hammond, Agua Caliente Cultural Museum
Cynthia Koch, Franklin D. Roosevelt Library-Museum
Beth Luey, Scholarly Publishing Program, Arizona State University
Karla Nicholson, Kentucky Historical Society
Lynne Poirier-Wilson, Asheville Art Museum & Independent Consultant
John Schleicher, Nebraska State Historical Society
Marjorie Schwarzer, Museum Studies, John F. Kennedy University
James Vaughan, National Trust for Historic Preservation
Lisa Watt, American Indian Museums Project/AASLH
Valerie Wheat, Museum Reference Center, Smithsonian Institution

ABOUT THE SERIES

The American Association for State and Local History Book Series publishes technical and professional information for those who practice and support history, and addresses issues critical to the field of state and local history. To submit a proposal or manuscript to the series, please request proposal guidelines from AASLH headquarters: AASLH Book Series, 1717 Church St., Nashville, Tennessee 37203. Telephone: (615) 320-3203. Fax: (615) 327-9013. Web site: www.aaslh.org.

ABOUT THE ORGANIZATION

The American Association for State and Local History (AASLH) is a nonprofit educational organization dedicated to advancing knowledge, understanding, and appreciation of local history in the United States and Canada. In addition to sponsorship of this book series, the Association publishes the periodical *History News*, a newsletter, technical leaflets and reports, and other materials; confers prizes and awards in recognition of outstanding achievement in the field; and supports a broad education program and other activities designed to help members work more effectively. To join the organization, contact: Membership Director, AASLH, 1717 Church St., Nashville, Tennessee 37203.

The Oral History Manual

Barbara W. Sommer
Mary Kay Quinlan

PRESS

A Division of
ROWMAN & LITTLEFIELD PUBLISHERS, INC.
Walnut Creek • Lanham • New York • Oxford

WINGATE UNIVERSITY LIBRARY

AltaMira Press
A Division of Rowman & Littlefield Publishers, Inc.
1630 North Main Street, #367
Walnut Creek, CA 94596
www.altamirapress.com

Rowman & Littlefield Publishers, Inc.
4720 Boston Way
Lanham, MD 20706

P.O. Box 317
Oxford OX2 9RU, England

Copyright © 2002 by AltaMira Press

All rights reserved. No part of this publication may be reproduced, stored in a retrieval system, or transmitted in any form or by any means, electronic, mechanical, photocopying, recording, or otherwise, without the prior permission of the publisher.

British Library Cataloguing in Publication Information Available

Library of Contress Cataloging-in-Publication Data

Sommer, Barbara W.
    The oral history manual / Barbara W. Sommer and Mary Kay Quinlan.
        p. cm.
    Includes bibliographical references and index.
    ISBN 0-7591-0100-0 (cloth : alk. paper) — ISBN 0-7591-0101-9 (pbk. : alk. paper)
    1. Oral history—Handbooks, manuals, etc. 2. Oral History—Methodology. 3. Interviewing—Handbooks, manuals, etc. 4. Historiography.   I. Quinlan, Mary Kay. II. Title.

D16.14.S69 2002
907'.2—dc21   2002008677

Printed in the United States of America

♾™ The paper used in this publication meets the minimum requirements of American National Standard for Information Sciences—Permanence of Paper for Printed Library Materials, ANSI/NISO Z39.48–1992.

Contents

Preface

People tell stories. Sometimes the stories begin "once upon a time," a signal to contemporary listeners that what they are about to hear is made up. A fairy tale. Fiction. Other times the storyteller—maybe your grandpa—begins: "Now this really happened. I know because I was there and I saw it with my own eyes." That's the stuff of oral history. And that's what this manual is designed to help readers collect. Not in the haphazard telling of stories around the Thanksgiving dinner table, where the eyewitness accounts sometimes blur into folk tales, but in a planned, organized, focused way that permits those who collect it today—and those who may use it decades from now—to glimpse and perhaps understand a time and place in the past through the words of those who experienced it firsthand.

This manual will take would-be oral historians systematically through the process of collecting oral histories, breaking the process down into steps that, if followed, will help assure a successful project. An oral history manual, however, cannot be like a cookbook, where following precise measurements of specific ingredients and combining them in prescribed ways usually results in a concoction quite similar to that depicted in the glossy photo accompanying the recipe.

Instead, this manual is more like a guide for making a quilt. It can tell would-be quilters what kinds of fabric work best, into what shapes and sizes the pieces should be cut, and the order in which they should be stitched together. But the resulting quilt will be unlike any other, its unique colors, fabrics, even its size reflecting the vision of the fiber artist who created it. And with its many small pieces stitched into a whole, a quilt offers its audience—those who see it on display as well as those who snuggle under it on a cold night—a kaleidoscopic image, changing with the light and with the perspective the audience brings.

Likewise, no two oral history projects will look alike, for their success depends on the vision of their creators and on how those oral historians apply the guidelines in this manual. And, like a quilt, the many historical voices an oral history project stitches together offer a kaleidoscopic view of a past time and place, a view that is preserved for another generation seeking a window on yesterday. For this reason, although we have included examples of some oral history projects in this manual, we have focused more on the steps needed to do a project. Our goal is to give you the tools you need to do your own successful project.

We owe a debt of gratitude to many people who made this manual possible. The Nebraska Humanities Council provided funding for early work that laid the foundation for this book, in collaboration with oral history colleague Robert Hurst, whose enthusiasm and dedication to oral history has contributed to this work. Terry Davis and Lauren Batte at the American Association for State and Local History likewise supported our efforts. We also count ourselves among the otherwise countless numbers of contemporary oral historians whose work relies on the expert guidance of books, pamphlets, and articles by John Neuenschwander and Donald A. Ritchie. Drafts of the manuscript improved thanks to the time and energy of Bruce Bruemmer, Carolyn Brown, Sara Collins, Paul Eisloeffel, Edward P. Nelson, and Fredene Pietsch, who read it and shared their constructive comments. Thanks also to Ann Quinlan and Eric Q. Mooring, who assisted with the illustrations. We are particularly grateful to Neuenschwander for leading us through the legal thicket and to Eisloeffel for helping us understand the intricacies of recording equipment and archival concerns.

Special thanks go to James E. Fogerty and Martha Ross, whose enthusiasm for oral history and willingness to teach others enfolded Sommer and Quinlan, respectively, into the oral history world and laid a rock-solid foundation. We are indebted to them for their continuing support.

Finally, we thank the hundreds of people who, collectively, have attended workshops we've taught, separately and together. Their ideas and questions have helped us refine our approach to teaching the techniques of oral history, which we have incorporated in this manual.

CHAPTER 1

Introduction

What do you think of when you hear the words "oral history"? Usually people define oral history as spoken stories about things that happened in the past. But confusion creeps in when you begin to refine the definition. Are family reminiscences oral history? What about oral traditions? Or journalists' stories about past events? What is the difference between each of these types of narratives and oral history? Or is there a difference?

Yes, there is. And this manual aims to help you learn about those differences and how to master the techniques of oral history. Certain processes for collecting first-hand, spoken narratives about the past clearly define oral history and set it apart from other interview methods. An oral history is created in a recorded interview setting, using a structured and well-researched interview outline, with a witness to or a participant in a historical event. Its aim is to collect and preserve the person's first-hand information and make it available to researchers. Careful attention to equipment selection, legal and ethical issues, and processing techniques characterizes the oral history process.

The key elements of oral history are:

- careful attention to copyright and other legal and ethical issues,
- a structured, well-researched interview format,
- a controlled, recorded interview setting,
- collection of first-hand information,
- use of high-quality sound or video equipment,
- adherence to careful processing techniques, and
- provisions for making interviews available at an accessible repository.

Oral history is most often done for one of two purposes: the desire to collect information that, in previous times, may have been part of a written record such as letters, diaries, or other "substantive and meaningful documents,"[1] or a determination to include many voices, not just the more powerful or dominant ones traditionally included in existing records. Thus oral historians look at their work as a way to complement and supplement the existing record, as well as a chance to make fundamental changes or additions to it.

Oral history does much more than document new information. It provides all those who use it a window to the past and, in doing so, makes history come alive. It reminds us that the actors are real people, each with a unique perspective on the past and present. It helps us understand not just what happened, but how those telling the story understood what happened and what they may now think of it. Exploring many sides of an issue through multiple first-hand individual accounts offers the opportunity to uncover layers of meaning embedded in the stories and insights into how people understand and interpret the past and their place in it.

Oral history is an interactive process involving several people—interviewer and narrator—operating within a defined structure. As such, it is not simply a statement of the narrator's knowledge, but a document that reflects the configuration of questions asked and responses given. Because of this, it is critically important that all steps taken to create and process an interview are thoroughly documented to help those using the information in the future understand the circumstances in which it was communicated.[2]

Using oral sources to obtain historical information is not new. Before written histories, societies usually relied on oral traditions, what Blackfeet Indian musician and poet Jack Gladstone calls the "living stories" repeated generation after generation. Oral traditions do not meet the definition of oral history because the narrators are not first-hand participants in the events they describe. But many scholars interested in such information use interviewing techniques similar to those of oral historians.

Folklorists also use similar field-interviewing techniques to obtain information. Whereas oral historians collect information about first-hand experiences, folklorists are more interested in traditional songs, stories, and other information, fact or fiction, about a community. Donald A. Ritchie, U.S. Senate associate historian, described the difference this

Figure 1.1. Oral history project materials. *Photo credit: Barbara W. Sommer.*

way: "An oral historian would most likely interview a husband and wife separately, seeking to identify the unique perspective of each spouse. A folklorist, being as interested in the way a story is told as in its substance, would interview the couple together to observe the interplay as one begins a story and the other finishes it."[3]

Oral history is sometimes confused with recording speeches or reading historical documents into a tape recorder. This is not oral history. Tape-recorded or videotaped reminiscences collected by turning on a tape recorder and asking Grandma to talk about the olden days are also often confused with oral history. In the absence of a structured interview, the thorough research necessary to prepare for the interview, emphasis on depth and detail of information collected, and adherence to strict processing techniques, reminiscences are not oral history.

People often think of journalistic interviews about historical topics as oral history. The difference is the purpose for which the materials are collected, their immediate intended use, and plans made for disposition and long-term availability of all original interview materials; these factors set oral history apart from journalistic interviews. The purpose of the oral history interview is to obtain detailed and lengthy responses to open-ended questions. The journalistic sound bite is not a part of the oral history process.

Oral history can help document much previously undocumented information about communities, organizations, businesses, events, or the lives of individuals. It can complement or supplement information already on the record, fill gaps in the historical record, bring out new and previously unknown information, help us understand how people view and understand the past, and, at times, correct or provide new insight into existing information or clarify confusing accounts. It can also uncover complexities and add new dimensions to what was generally perceived as a simple, straightforward recitation of past events.

Oral history interviews generally can be grouped into two categories: life interviews and oral history projects. Both use oral history techniques but have somewhat different focuses. Life interviews usually involve multiple interview sessions with one person to create a collection of autobiographical materials. An oral history project, on the other hand, usually focuses on an event, place, or topic. It is a series of oral history interviews with a variety of individuals about a specific historical topic of in-

terest. Both techniques highlight the value of oral history. Creating a number of interviews about one person, subject, or topic, designed to complement one another, can provide a depth and breadth of information not often found in other primary sources.

Oral history projects are often used to document events in the history of a community. The broader applications of life interviews, which are often created for family or genealogical purposes, are, however, sometimes overlooked. These interviews can contain valuable information about community history. So even if your immediate interest is documenting the life of a family member or an individual, the procedures outlined in this manual make it possible for others outside the family to benefit from the information you will collect. The same is true about the broader aspects of community history. While information collected may be of interest to a local area, its contribution to greater understanding of related state and national issues should not be overlooked. Local perspectives often provide insight into state and national issues that cannot be found anywhere else. For example, documentation through oral history interviews of one High Plains community's response to race relations, missile locations during the Cold War, upheaval in the farm economy, and changes in people's perceptions of Main Street, while important to an understanding of the community itself, provide invaluable grass-roots insight into issues of national importance.

Oral history also serves communities with a history of disenfranchisement. Those with little or no written record, or for whom the written record is distorted at best, benefit greatly from the use of oral history. In many cases, while documenting the community's history is critical in itself, the interview also becomes a catalyst. It can provide an avenue to correct long-held misconceptions about an event or a time period. It can help collect information that balances the existing record. It can become an impetus for developing community pride through the telling of a community's story in its own words. It can be a tool to save the vernacular, or in the case of Native Americans, rapidly vanishing languages. Oral history projects, with their emphasis on personal outreach, can benefit the entire community by bringing people together—narrators with interviewers and others interested in the work of the project.

An example of the role oral history can play is found in *A Guide for Oral History in the Native American Community*. The authors of the document—leaders of a several-decades-old project among the Suquamish people of the northwestern United States—devote an entire chapter to the importance of oral history to their tribal community. They describe the benefits as "not only a successful project of documentation, but also one of cultural renewal."[4] The benefits include supporting creation of an oral history archives, development of much-needed educational materials, and providing opportunities for higher education through work-study positions developed as part of the project. But the benefits go beyond this. Project leaders cite more subjective factors such as instilling youth with pride in their Native American identities and maintaining pride among elders through involvement in projects that perpetuate tribal heritage (creating a program for elders to work as VISTA volunteers on local cultural programs and arranging for elders to serve as "foster grandparents" in local schools). Other equally important benefits include encouraging ongoing ties among community members, such as sponsoring a regular elders luncheon through which many of the oral history contacts are made, providing outreach and companionship to tribal elders, and asking interviewers to serve as liaison between elders and tribal social and health services programs.

In such cases, an oral history project becomes an integral part of the community. In all cases, regardless of the type of role a project plays in community organization, it becomes a vehicle for documenting not only facts about the past, but also the more subjective insights into how people organize their views of their history and how their frames of reference in their own communities as well as in the dominant communities affect their sense of the events discussed in an interview.

Who participates in an oral history interview? The interview usually has two participants, the interviewer, who is the oral historian, and the narrator, sometimes called the interviewee or chronicler or informant. For clarity's sake, this manual calls the person being interviewed the narrator. The interviewer is responsible for carrying out the interview. The narrator is chosen for his or her first-hand knowledge about a certain subject and for the ability to communicate this knowledge effectively.

Oral history depends on memory and the ability to communicate information clearly. Skeptics sometimes question the content of an interview as too subjective to be reliable. Yet oral historians have found that well-prepared interviewers who have done the necessary background research and have developed organized interview outlines can obtain information that helps add substantive new material and new perspectives to the historical record. As with information from other primary and secondary sources, the information in an oral history interview adds to our understanding of the past. And the first-person accounts add an immediacy that rarely can be found in other sources.

The interaction between the interviewer and the narrator affects the interview. This is inevitable. It is a part of the oral history process. Unlike the diarist who privately records information of his or her own choosing, the narrator who participates in an oral history interview provides information and insights in collaboration with an interviewer who has chosen the narrator specifically because of the information or perspective he or she can provide. The interviewer guides the discussion and helps clarify information, which the narrator provides in his or her own words. This makes the interviewer an integral part of the process, emphasizing the need for interviewers to take their responsibilities very seriously. It also emphasizes the importance of fully documenting the entire interview development process so that future users of the materials understand the context within which the interview was created.

Mining a narrator's memory to obtain information is a fascinating process that takes time and patience. People often forget details. Memories can become blurred. During the interview, however, the narrator usually concentrates fully on the events being documented. This, coupled with well-framed questions that can include the mention of already documented facts learned through background research, can remind the narrator of information he or she might not remember in casual conversation or reminiscences. Anyone who has completed an oral history interview and heard the narrator say "I remembered more than I ever thought I would" knows that preparation, patience, and willingness to work with the narrator can help bring back long-forgotten details. And a well-researched, well-structured interview is critical to making that happen.

Oral history interviews can cover events that happened a long time ago and are thus filtered through memory and the passage of time, or they can cover more recent events. In the latter case, the information gathered is more direct and immediate. People may, however, refuse to talk about certain events shortly after they happen, especially if the memories are traumatic. The timing of a project or the request for an interview, therefore, may have an effect on the results. That's why it is important for oral historians to document thoroughly the circumstances of the interview. This documentation provides the context within which the interview occurred and can be an invaluable aid to future researchers interested in using the material.

Oral historians need to be sensitive to the needs of the narrator and knowledgeable about the oral history process. Not only will this help make a project or a series of life interviews go more smoothly, it will also help produce an interview that contains clearly articulated information and deals as effectively as possible with the subjectivity and individuality of memory.

Oral history represents one of many ways to document the past. Each way has its strengths. Oral history brings an immediacy and an ability to explore subjective nuances to a study of the past. When developed properly, it is a valuable tool for historians. It allows researchers to probe beneath the surface of the written record to discover not just what happened but how and why, to explain anomalies, to provide convincing evidence or tantalizing clues that enhance understanding of a past time and place. Through it, information that otherwise might have been lost can be collected and preserved as primary source material for researchers. And a sense of the richness of the human experience can be passed to future generations. Moreover, a well-planned and well-executed oral history project can strengthen an organization and bring people together as they collectively work to understand more about the past.

Historians are not the only practitioners of oral history. It is also used in the classroom as a teaching technique. Educators like it because of its interdisciplinary nature, drawing on a variety of research, verbal, writing, and technical skills, and its built-in ability to tie the school to the community in a unique way. Gerontologists also often use oral history techniques. Working with elderly people, they use life review techniques as therapy. In both cases, although working toward a specific end, the information collected can serve a broader purpose by providing insight into the history of a community. Following the procedures in this manual can help make it possible for others to benefit from such information.

Many books provide background about oral history, ranging from practical discussions of its applications to theoretical analyses of the use of memory as a research technique. Examples of these works are listed in the bibliography.

The Oral History Association (OHA) is also a source of information about oral history. Its purpose is to bring together people from many professions and disciplines who share a common interest in oral history and to encourage excellence in its collection, preservation, dissemination, and interpretation. The Oral History Association also publishes materials to help practitioners. The *Oral History Review*, which OHA members receive, contains articles about oral history along with media reviews and review essays. The *OHA Newsletter*, published three times a year, contains information about the organization and its members. First issued in 1968 and regularly updated, the OHA *Evaluation Guidelines* were written to promote professional standards for oral historians. They are organized in checklist form and offer reminders of the issues involved in conducting, processing, and preserving oral history interviews. Not every project or series of life interviews will make use of every guideline, but taken together, the guidelines provide a basis for more fully understanding the professional standards in the field of oral history. The complete text of the *Evaluation Guidelines: Principles and Standards of the Oral History Association* is included in appendix 7.

Several other historical organizations also have guidelines that govern the conduct of members. Although not all mention oral history specifically, the guidelines define a standard for working in the history and museum fields, which often includes the collection of oral history. Collectively, they support the goal of working to the highest standards of the profession.

One important guide is the American Association for State and Local History (AASLH) "Statement of Professional Ethics." AASLH is dedicated to serving all facets of the field of history. As such it serves many people and agencies that incorporate the use of oral history into their programs. This ethics statement, developed for the AASLH membership with its variety of disciplines and professions, defines the standards expected of those associated with the organization. Although not specifically focused on oral history, it reinforces the standards and ethics for those who work with history and its stories of the past.

This manual takes a step-by-step approach to help anyone interested in oral history learn how to plan and carry out a project effectively. It explains what works and why. And if you get hooked on oral history—as untold numbers of people have—it offers resources for more ideas on creating and using oral histories.

Notes

1. Carol Kammen and Norma Prendergast, *Encyclopedia of Local History* (Walnut Creek, Calif.: AltaMira Press, 2000), 357.

2. For further reading on oral history, its uses and interpretations, please see David K. Dunaway and Willa K. Baum, *Oral History: An Interdisciplinary Anthology*, 2d ed. (Walnut Creek, Calif.: AltaMira Press, 2000); Paul Thompson, *The Voice of the Past: Oral History*, 3d ed. (Oxford: Oxford University Press, 2000); Roy Rosenzweig and David Thelen, *The Presence of the Past: Popular Uses of History in American Life* (New York: Columbia University Press, 1998); and Carol Kammen, *On Doing Local History: Reflections on What Local Historians Do, Why, and What It Means* (Walnut Creek, Calif.: AltaMira Press, 1986).

3. Donald A. Ritchie, *Doing Oral History* (New York: Twayne Publishers, 1995), 16.

4. Suquamish Oral History Project, *A Guide for Oral History in the Native American Community*, 3d ed. (Suquamish: Suquamish Tribal Cultural Center, 2000), 5.

CHAPTER 2

Project Overview and Planning

Why are people interested in oral history? Why do they do it? Oral history can add vibrant, first-hand accounts of events or people to the historical record and allows you to probe a narrator's memory to clarify information about the past. For example:

- **Historical organizations** and other institutions often find oral history is an excellent way to collect primary source information about a subject either forgotten or neglected by the written record. It can be used to correct misinterpretations or to fill in gaps about subjects for which limited materials exist. In addition, because of its inherent grass-roots nature, it often becomes an excellent tie between institution and community. The size of the institution need not matter. Organizations as large as state historical societies and as small as local, volunteer-run county historical societies and public libraries have active oral history programs.

- **Communities**, in the most general sense of the word, use oral history for many of the same reasons. It provides an opportunity to document information that otherwise would be lost. Projects can focus on cities, neighborhoods, or particular segments of a community, such as women's groups or ethnic groups. Organizations use it to document their histories and, in some cases, the history of change in the professions they represent. Any community institution, such as a business, church, library, school, or volunteer organization, can effectively use oral history.

- **Teachers**, looking at its interdisciplinary possibilities and as an innovative way to meet state standards, incorporate oral history into curricula, giving students the experience of creating primary source materials while promoting closer relations between school and community. The subjects they choose range from the history of the school to a closer look at a particular event or topic in the community's history.

- **Government agencies** sometimes use oral history as a way of adding to the historical record by collecting unwritten insight into various actions and decisions. Most of the presidential libraries also have active oral history programs, as do the branches of the armed services and many governmental agencies.

- Some institutions have **ongoing oral history programs** that are an integral part of their operations. This is most often found at state historical societies and universities. Among the most notable are the Minnesota Historical Society, the Idaho Historical Society, and the Montana Historical Society. Well-established university programs are found at Columbia University, the University of California at Los Angeles, the University of California, Berkeley, and Baylor University, among others. Many other colleges and universities develop specific projects when support is available.

- **Families** sometimes use oral history to document the lives of their members.

- **Public and private institutions and organizations** also use oral history to collect information about major figures, such as a governor or another prominent political leader. This can be done both through a series of life interviews and by talking to people who knew the person. Some projects include a mixture of the two approaches.

Uses of oral history are limited only by imagination and by the foresight of those who organize a project. Whether created by institutions or individuals, oral history projects become a source of pride to all involved and to their sponsors and practitioners.

When thinking about oral history, people often confuse the interview with the entire oral history process. The interview is the vehicle by which the oral history information is collected. As such it is a critical part of the process. But it is only a part of the process. Its success is based on the project planning work that precedes it and the processing work that follows it. Without this, the opportunity for in-depth inquiry that makes an oral history interview an exciting and vital primary source document can be lost, as can access to the information in it.

Whether you choose a life history or a topical oral history project, careful planning and organization are key to success. Although it may not seem important to methodically go through the steps of planning a project, doing so can make or break it. Planning helps focus the work. Who is it being done for and why? What topics will and will not be included in the interviews and why? What information already exists and what does it tell us? Who will own the final product? These are critical questions that will affect the final product.

The planning process also may open new and otherwise unrealized avenues of inquiry. It can help identify information that otherwise might have been missed and will help determine the importance of including this information as an interview topic. It may lead to the discovery that what seemed like a simple little project to interview a handful of people could become a much more exciting project somewhat broader in scope with the opportunity to collect fascinating and useful information.

Working through each of the planning steps in the development of an oral history project or a series of life interviews will help solidify the work and clarify its purpose. Doing so increases the probability for strong, focused, and well-thought-out interviews.

Sometimes a project starts with little more than the intuitive sense that a particular person in the community—often an elderly person—is a storehouse of otherwise unrecorded information about an important event or time in the community's past. If that's the case, you might start with a preliminary planning project to become familiar with the oral history process and develop several sample or trial interviews. Following the project planning steps outlined below can encourage planners to focus on the goals, processes, and resources needed to make a larger project successful. Starting small with a preliminary planning project also can help develop themes or topics, identify a pool of possible narrators, and attract funds to support a larger project.

The following steps outline the oral history planning process. Each one is important to a project's success. Subsequent chapters explain each step in detail.

IDENTIFY KEY LEADERS AND PROJECT PERSONNEL

The first step in an oral history project is a basic one—find people to help carry it out. This does not yet mean the people to be interviewed. When beginning a project, the first step is to recruit project coordinators. This is critical. As with any project, the need for several people to accept responsibility for leadership can mean the difference between success and failure. You should also begin to think about other people you will need to carry out the project, such as project interviewers and transcribers or tape indexers. Interviewers may help plan the project, but this isn't necessary. With project leaders in place, you're ready to move on to the next planning steps.

NAME THE PROJECT

This name is the one by which the project will be known while it's under way and after it's completed. If project letterhead or business cards are printed, the name can and should be used on these materials. It helps give the project definition and a clear identity.

WRITE A MISSION STATEMENT

This task involves semantics. It may sound easy but is often one of the more difficult assignments in developing a project. A mission statement should be only a few sentences long and should clearly answer the question, What are we trying to accomplish? Appendix 4 contains sample wording.

DECIDE WHO WILL OWN PROJECT MATERIALS

This means choosing a repository. It is an important decision, for it determines who will own copyright. With ownership comes an ongoing responsibility for care of all products of the project, including permanent storage of cassettes or discs and transcripts, and provision of access to researchers. It is a responsibility not to be taken lightly. Historical societies, libraries, and schools often develop or sponsor oral history projects. In such cases, ownership of the products is probably easily determined. In other cases, you will have to approach an institution and discuss possible ownership. Do this as early in project planning as possible.

DETERMINE THE EQUIPMENT TO USE IN THE INTERVIEWS AND IN TRANSCRIBING

This will provoke lively discussion and is one of the larger expenses in developing a project. Equipment decisions include whether to use audio or video, how to combine the two if both are to be used, and what types of equipment will produce final products that best fit the budget and serve the project's needs.

DEVELOP A PROJECT BUDGET

Oral history is an exciting and invigorating process. But the reality of financial needs can stop a good project before it gets off the ground. It helps to create a budget early in the planning process and to include all possible project costs. With this, you can begin to determine realistically what you can and cannot accomplish. The costs of developing and carrying out an oral history project are often underestimated, which can lead to difficulties. Mapping out expected costs early in the project helps everyone understand its needs.

FIND FUNDING SOURCES

This can be an ongoing process because oral history projects take time and therefore can be expensive. Unless full funding already exists, laying the groundwork for obtaining funding should start as soon as you have defined the project and developed a budget.

SELECT A PROJECT ADVISORY BOARD

This is a way to build a network of support for a project. The people on the advisory board are not responsible for the intensive planning work. They might be community leaders who will help find funding sources or equipment when needed. They might be experts on the general subject of the interviews or those with a good grounding in history, chosen to help guide the project on the most effective use of its time and resources. A liaison with a sponsoring institution also often serves on this board. Choose advisory board members for the support they can give to the project or their access to the types of expertise the project needs.

An advisory board does not have to meet regularly. Often a meeting at the beginning of the project is sufficient with periodic follow-up reports to let board members know how the project is progressing. Some boards also meet when the project is completed to help celebrate the results. If appropriate, individual advisory board members may be asked to be available to answer questions or to help with a particular phase of the project.

ESTABLISH A TIME FRAME FOR COMPLETING THE PROJECT

Blocks of time should be defined for various project tasks. The time it takes to adequately prepare for the interviews, acquire good equipment, do the interviews, and process them effectively can take its toll on even the most enthusiastic project participants. Developing a time frame at this point helps you think through the project, identifying the necessary tasks and the time that can realistically be allotted to complete each one. Laying out expectations, even if they change during the project, can help everyone better understand its needs.

ESTABLISH RECORD-KEEPING PROCEDURES

Be sure to designate someone to handle general administrative responsibilities for the project. Duties include making sure all project forms are organized and available, creating procedures to track the status of interviews, and providing for transcription and processing of project interviews. Standard project paperwork includes the donor or legal release form, a biographical information form, and an interview information form.

As discussed further in chapter 3, the donor or legal release form provides for transfer of copyright to the repository you've designated to hold the interview materials. This allows future researchers to have access to the interview information. It is an essential part of the support materials for an interview and must be signed if the interview is to become part of the available primary source materials in the repository's collections. It should be filled out and signed after each interview, even if another interview is planned with the same narrator. Failure to do so leaves ownership of the interview with those whose voices are on the tape. This is confusing at best and leads to a muddled mess as time goes on.

The biographical information form gathers background information about the narrator, while the interview information form contains the interview abstract and is the first step in making interview content accessible to researchers. Sample forms are found in appendix 2.

DEVELOP A PUBLICITY PLAN

Project publicity includes everything from letting people know it is taking place to encouraging use of the completed interviews. Publicity will help all steps of the project by encouraging support—financial and material—and maintaining participant and community enthusiasm.

TRAIN YOUR INTERVIEWERS

Unless your project plans to hire experienced oral historians to conduct interviews, training interviewers is integral to a project's success. Project coordinators may schedule an initial training session followed by several additional sessions scheduled throughout the course of the project to help interviewers hone their skills.

By following these steps, you've now laid the groundwork for your project. The next section outlines the research necessary for successful oral history interviews. The research itself is a two-step process: general research about the subject of your oral history project and specific research about the background and role of each narrator you plan to interview.

BEGIN BACKGROUND RESEARCH ON THE PROJECT TOPIC AND COMPILE A BIBLIOGRAPHY

Research builds the foundation for good interviews. Begin by identifying existing sources of information about the topic to clarify what information is available and what is lacking. This helps you determine where and how oral history will be most useful. Books, newspapers, diaries, letters, and maps are all potential sources of information on your topic and may lead you to other materials as well. Some might be easier to find than others, but it is important to identify key information about the topic at the beginning of the project.

Keep careful research records, documenting every item used, and be sure sources are clearly identified. This information becomes support material for the interviews, helping future researchers understand why and how the interviews were developed as they were. Careful work at this point will save immeasurable time in later stages of the project.

USE THE RESEARCH TO CREATE AN OUTLINE RELATING TO THE TOPIC

This outline should list basic benchmarks identified in the research including dates, names, important facts, and any major events that will help in developing the project. It creates a structure for continued research and will be an important part of interviewer training materials and preparation for the interviews.

MAKE A LIST OF THEMES OR TOPICS TO PURSUE IN THE INTERVIEWS

This list should be based on the research and may focus on gaps or contradictions in the existing record. It may also include ideas for reflective questions. With this, the oral history interviews begin to take shape.

IDENTIFY POTENTIAL NARRATORS AND DETERMINE THE TOPICS OR THEMES TO BE COVERED IN INTERVIEWS WITH EACH OF THEM

As your project evolves, think in terms of the information you're trying to collect rather than the number of people you want to interview. Focusing on numbers of people can move the project away from its focus. Instead, focus on the themes you want to cover and who among potential narrators has the appropriate information about these themes.

The names of project narrators will come from a variety of sources and will probably begin to come in as soon as you announce you are doing a project. Suggestions will be made by people involved with the project, people who learn about it through other sources, and from the research. As names are suggested, fill out a Potential Narrator Information Form for each person (sample in appendix 2). Include the name, address, and phone number of each person and notes about what they know, how their knowledge can contribute to the project's goals, and how and when they would be available to be interviewed. Realizing that the number of potential narrators will grow as the project continues and more names surface, this becomes the potential narrator pool.

You will want to include narrators from a variety of backgrounds and those who represent all sides of the issues to make sure the interview topics are documented as thoroughly and accurately as possible. As you work through this step, you will also want to match potential narrators to your project topics. This will help you determine how many narrators you need and will help maintain a narrator balance on all sides of issues.

When you reach this point, you will want to begin thinking about whom to interview. It is helpful to set interviewing priorities based on your needs and goals and on the knowledge and availability of narrators. Narrators' ages and health are also often issues. As you start making decisions, begin to make initial contact with the first narrators, asking each to participate in the project. This is usually done by letter with a telephone call as a follow-up. Sending a letter first gives the person time to think through the possibility of being interviewed and to formulate questions about the project. The follow-up telephone call provides an opportunity for the narrator to talk with a project representative, asking any questions he or she may have. A sample contact letter is included in appendix 3.

BEGIN NARRATOR-SPECIFIC RESEARCH

Now you've completed the general background research and you're ready to move into the interviewing phase of the project. Each interview is based on specific research. This research builds on the more general project research done earlier. It provides the structure for the interview and is some of the most important work of the project. Through it, the interviewer learns about the narrator and begins to develop the interview outline.

The specific research phase must be as thorough as possible. It is done by the interviewer whenever possible and should include a review of written sources and, depending on circumstances, can include visits to places related to the interview topics or themes. Through this research, interviewers will familiarize themselves with the project's topics or themes as well as the narrator's experiences and knowledge about these topics or themes.

Although interviewers will be eager to begin the interviews, resist the temptation to rush this phase of the project. A well-prepared interviewer will make the difference between a superficial interview and one that has the depth and breadth of good oral history. Taking the time to prepare thoroughly for the interview is one of the interviewer's most important responsibilities. This requires patience and a willingness to make the time to do the thorough research necessary to be properly grounded in the topics that will be covered in the interview.

DEVELOP THE INTERVIEW OUTLINE

This is the list of specific topics and themes that will be covered in the interview. It is not a scripted list of questions, but should contain information that will form the basis for interview questions. It also can include information the interviewer may want to refer to or quote from during the interview. It is the interview's road map. A sample interview guide is included in appendix 5.

SCHEDULE THE INTERVIEW

This is usually done by a telephone call to the narrator, following initial written correspondence to introduce the project and invite the narrator to participate. A pre-interview may also be scheduled at this time to allow narrator and interviewer to meet. This can be helpful, though the interviewer will want to make sure the narrator does not prematurely begin to launch into his or her stories. Whether over the telephone or in person, many interviewers use this contact to obtain biographical information about the narrator as well.

CONDUCT THE INTERVIEW

This is the centerpiece of an oral history project: the interview through which the narrator's information is recorded. It is *not* a dialogue or a conversation in which both parties equally share their views. The role of the interviewer is to guide the interview, asking clear, open-ended questions that encourage the narrator to tell his or her story. A good oral history interview consists of open-ended questions followed by long answers containing as much detail as the narrator can remember. At the end of the interview, both narrator and interviewer should sign the legal release form.

PROCESS THE MATERIALS

These are the steps you'll take to make information in the interview accessible. The first step should be to fill out an Interview Information Form (see example in appendix 2). By noting who the interviewer and narrator are, the date of the interview and signing of the legal release form, and the number and type of recording media used, and by including a short summary of the interview, this form gives immediate control over the interview products and information. If at all possible, the next processing step should include full transcription. Although a written transcript is one step removed from the original recording with its nuances of voice and pronunciation, it helps make the interview information easily accessible to researchers. Reading a transcript does not preclude listening to the interview to obtain additional insight into the subject.

Transcribing takes time but planning for it will benefit the project in the long run. If you cannot arrange for transcription, creating a timed tape log is essential. Although it is not as complete as a transcript and is dependent on the user being able to listen to a copy of the recording to obtain information, it provides access to the interview. Transcript and tape log samples are included in appendix 6.

After completing a project, many coordinators have a celebration, inviting all who were involved to thank them for their time and participation. You can also give each narrator a copy of the cassettes or discs and transcript from his or her interview.

These often become treasured family keepsakes.

The rest of this manual provides detailed information about each of the oral history planning steps outlined here. You can accomplish some of these steps with a phone call or a short meeting. Others are more complicated and will take considerable time and effort. Following the steps carefully will result in a strong project, however, while skimping on any of them is sure to cause problems as the project evolves.

For further information about project planning and development, see *Doing Oral History* by Donald A. Ritchie (full citation in the bibliography).

Legal and Ethical Considerations

What legal and ethical considerations apply to the practice of oral history?

Oral history projects often are born of a desire to capture the memories of elderly community members or to increase knowledge about places or historic events. But enthusiastic planners often have no idea they're embarking on a project with important legal and ethical dimensions. This chapter will:

- introduce the basic legal and ethical considerations that underpin oral history practice;
- discuss how legal and ethical issues affect project planning and administration, equipment decisions, processing, and the end use of the oral history interview; and
- discuss the legal and ethical dimensions of rapidly changing technology and financial issues that affect oral history practice.

But this chapter will not:

- offer a shortcut to law school;
- provide legal advice;
- discuss unique requirements imposed by federal regulation on oral history work in colleges and universities or other research institutions; and
- recommend archives management policies. Many legal and ethical considerations affect procedures for handling interview tapes and transcripts. While this chapter will describe the range of issues and options to consider, it is no substitute for professional archival information, which can be obtained from qualified archivists. The Society of American Archivists and the American Association for State and Local History are good sources of information about archives management issues.

The primary legal framework for oral history work rests on the established legal premise that an oral history interview creates a copyrightable document as soon as the recorder is turned off at the end of an interview session. You should decide during the planning process how to secure copyright (the exclusive legal right to reproduce, distribute, display, perform, or create derivative works) from the interview's creators and how to responsibly handle the materials your project creates. This chapter will help you accomplish that.

Oral histories came to be treated as copyrightable documents in the earliest days of institutional oral history practice at Columbia University where the interviews or oral memoirs were deemed analogous to written autobiographies, which authors clearly could copyright. Over time, the practice evolved of asking narrators to give their copyright interest to institutions sponsoring oral history programs, thus alleviating the need for the narrators themselves to control access to the materials. Narrators or interviewers legally could insist on retaining their copyright interest and simply grant project sponsors permission to use their interviews in specific ways—with or without certain restrictions. Indeed, the Library of Congress' Veterans History Project, which aims to create a massive online collection of interviews with veterans, requires narrators and interviewers to sign donor forms giving the project ownership and unrestricted authorization to use the interviews while technically allowing narrators and interviewees to retain copyright interest. While the donor forms give the Library of Congress carte blanche permission to use and distribute the interviews, anyone other than the Library who wanted to use them would have to seek out the narrators and interviewers or their heirs to get permission to do so. Such situations are cumbersome at best.

The Veterans History Project approach to the copyright issue is atypical. Institutions that sponsor oral history programs or repositories that include oral histories in their collections typically hold the copyright for those materials and are responsible for making them accessible under whatever conditions they deem appropriate, subject to any restrictions noted on the donor forms. Transfer of copyright is consistent with the legal and ethical standards promulgated by the Oral History Association (OHA), the national professional organization of oral history practitioners. Moreover, most institutions or organizations that sponsor or maintain oral history collections would be reluctant to accept interviews without clear legal rights to use them and make them accessible to others, which a copyright transfer insures. While rare situations might occur, such as a highly prominent narrator who insisted on having an intellectual property lawyer negotiate a unique donor form, the vast majority of oral history interviews do not fall into that category. Customized donor forms for each interview in a collection would be an archivist's nightmare, and management issues associated with such one-of-a-kind legal documents should be considered carefully in a project's planning stages.

Indeed, a host of legal and ethical issues arises at virtually every stage of creating an oral history. In its publication *Evaluation Guidelines: Principles and Standards of the Oral History Association*, the OHA describes the ethical principles and standards that should guide oral historians. (The complete text of that publication is included in appendix 7.) These principles and standards outline an oral historian's responsibilities to narrators, to the public, and to the profession and the responsibilities of institutions that sponsor oral history programs or serve as repositories for collections of oral history materials.

The ethical framework that the OHA describes is based on these premises:

- Narrators invited to be interviewed for a project should fairly reflect all sides of the topic or issue being pursued.

- A narrator is entitled to respect for his or her story, even if it differs markedly from customary interpretations of an event.

- A narrator must give fully informed consent to participate in an oral history interview. Full information includes a thorough description of the purposes of the project as well as the expected disposition and dissemination of the materials.

- An interviewer should be well trained, for only a competent interviewer who has prepared thoroughly will be able to conduct an interview that goes beyond superficial treatment of the topic and results in the collection of new information of lasting value.

- An interviewer should document fully the preparation, methods, and circumstances of an interview, for only with such background information can future users of the interview make informed judgments about its content.

- Rewards and recognition that come to an oral history project should be shared with narrators and their communities.

- Whoever owns the final product, whether an individual or an institution, should maintain the highest professional standards in preserving the oral history interviews and making them available to others.

If you're planning an oral history project, become thoroughly familiar with the OHA *Evaluation Guidelines* before starting. You also should study *Oral History and the Law*, by John A. Neuenschwander,[1] a past OHA president, history professor, lawyer, and municipal judge. Published by the OHA as part of its pamphlet series, *Oral History and the Law* is the single, most complete source of information about this topic. It provides considerably more detail about legal issues potentially affecting oral historians than this manual can offer, and it should be a part of every oral historian's library. But even it is not a substitute for competent legal advice, which all projects should seek during the planning stages as a way to prevent legal problems down the road. Project coordinators should provide their institution's legal staff with copies of the OHA pamphlet, too.

The rest of this manual describes in detail the steps necessary to create an oral history project. The remainder of this chapter outlines the legal and ethical issues you should consider at each step.

PLANNING A PROJECT

The first—and most important—legal issue project coordinators must address is who will own the materials the project ultimately creates. While it may seem premature to think about what should be done with materials that don't yet exist, it is fundamental to the rest of the planning process because it determines who will hold the copyright to the oral history interviews, maintain the materials, and govern access to them.

Because an oral history interview is a copyrightable document from the moment the interview ends, both interviewer and narrator—and anyone else whose voice is on the tape—have a copyright interest in the material on the recording. No one else may use it without their permission. Thus, to make the oral history interviews readily available for

The donor form transfers copyright to the designated owner. Always remember the narrator and the interviewer should sign the donor form after each interview.

researchers and others to use, both interviewer and narrator should sign a donor or legal release form at the end of each interview session giving their copyright interest to the project.

PROJECT ADMINISTRATION

Handling the paperwork an oral history project generates is an ongoing responsibility of project coordinators. Perhaps the single most important piece of paper associated with oral history projects is the donor form or legal release form, which gives the project repository (the place that owns and maintains the materials) the right to use and disseminate the oral history materials. Unless the project has a signed release form that properly transfers copyright for each oral history interview, public access to the information would be possible only if the narrators and interviewers or their heirs granted permission to specific requests for access, a prospect most repositories would deem impractical and unworkable. Equally impractical from a repository's standpoint would be donor forms in which the narrator retained copyright but authorized the repository to use the material only in certain ways.

If you're working with a repository that already has an oral history collection, the repository itself likely will dictate the nature of the donor form required. If, however, the oral history materials will be held by an institution unfamiliar with such release forms, you'll need to write one, with the advice of informed legal counsel. It should be noted that oral history might be an unfamiliar concept to many lawyers. You'll need to be prepared to explain thoroughly what you are doing and provide relevant materials, such as Neuenschwander's pamphlet, available through the OHA. Above all, be prepared to insist that any documents narrators and interviewers are asked to sign be written in commonly understood language, not legalistic mumbo jumbo. Narrators cannot give informed consent if they cannot understand the document they're asked to sign. Simple, one-page forms are the best. Sample release forms can be found in appendix 2. Other samples are included in *Oral History and the Law*.

These sample forms can be a useful guide, but resist the temptation merely to copy these release forms or forms from another oral history project. Instead, be sure the donor agreement you use meets *your* project's needs.

A donor form can be either a contract or a deed of gift. To be complete legally and, thus, enforceable, each of these documents must contain specific elements discussed briefly below. The key distinction between the two is that a contract must provide for what is known legally as "consideration" or payment. Some oral history projects use a contract form, stipulating, for example, a token payment of one dollar or promising the narrator a bound copy of the interview transcript. Considerably more common is the deed of gift form, a voluntary transfer of property without any payment. Indeed, some projects call their donor form a "gift of personal memoir." Be sure you don't create a hybrid donor form that includes elements of both a contract and a deed of gift. Such hybrids are more difficult to defend legally because they fall outside the boundaries of the conventional legal framework.

Whatever form you use, it should include:

- clear identification of the name of the narrator;
- clear identification of the project repository;
- a statement that the narrator is transferring "legal title and all literary property rights to the interview, including copyright" to the repository;
- a place for the narrator to sign; and
- a place for the interviewer to sign.

Federal copyright law specifies that for a copyright transfer to be valid, it must be in writing and signed by the copyright owner. So be sure the donor form contains a specific reference to copyright, and not some generic, legal-sounding language about "all rights, title and interest."

Donor forms also may include restrictions on how interviews may or may not be used. Such restrictions might allow use of the material in various formats for nonprofit use, but prohibit use of the materials for commercial purposes without the narrator's written consent or that of their heirs. Try to resist the temptation to create overly specific lists of possible future uses of the material, which run the risk of creating an inflexible project that legally cannot be used in creative new formats.

Of particular concern in recent years is the proliferation of oral history projects that choose to put materials on the Internet. While the ethical arguments over the merits of Internet dissemination of oral history materials are discussed below, any project that contemplates doing so should include in its donor form a specific reference to electronic distribution as well as archival deposit and copyright.

While holding the copyright to the oral history materials might clearly give a project the legal right to put materials online, most oral historians would consider it a serious breach of ethics to do so unless narrators were fully informed about the intent to do so and agreed to it in advance. Many oral history collections now considering Internet dissemination of materials face the daunting prospect of retroactively seeking permission from narrators (or their heirs) whose memories were recorded long before the digital age. So even if project coordinators don't currently plan electronic distribution of oral history materials, they should consider including a specific reference allowing it to alleviate future complications. Narrators always may stipulate that they do not wish such distribution of an interview, which should be noted clearly in the signed legal agreement.

Other unusual situations occasionally occur that will affect the donor form. As you plan your project, consider possibilities such as those discussed below and decide how to handle them should they arise.

- Narrators—or interviewers—who are reluctant to assign copyright to the project because they want to use the material for their own written memoirs or other work before the interviews are opened to the general public. You can handle this dilemma by including a sentence in your donor forms stipulating that the narrator or interviewer has the right to first use of the material for a specified period of time. This amounts to the copyright holder—the project's sponsor—granting a license for use of the material. Alternatively, language could be included stipulating that the gift of copyright doesn't preclude use of the interview itself by the narrator or interviewer. These kinds of situations call for careful consultation with the project's legal adviser to arrive at language that meets everyone's needs.

- Narrators who want to close access to all or part of their interviews. This usually occurs when a narrator has something unflattering, highly controversial, or potentially defamatory to say about someone. Such information can be important to the interview because of the context it provides, and, in these unusual circumstances, an oral history project may agree to close access to the interview materials for a specified number of years or until the death of the parties named in the interview. Defamation issues will be discussed more fully below in connection with processing and archiving oral history materials. But you should understand—and should make sure narrators understand—that while materials can be closed to researchers, they are unlikely to be protected from subpoena. As Neuenschwander has repeatedly noted, U.S. courts generally have not recognized an archival privilege or scholar's privilege analogous to the legal protections that apply to communications between husbands and wives or doctors and patients. Similarly, state and federal open records laws can affect the ability of a project sponsored by a government agency to restrict access to oral history materials. Open records laws vary, so you'll need to determine what conditions prevail in your jurisdiction. A sample of a restricted donor form is included in appendix 2.

- Narrators who wish to remain anonymous. Oral history projects occasionally seek interviews with AIDS patients, battered women, drug addicts, or members of political, religious, or other groups who fear persecution for sharing their life stories. If your project entertains the notion of interviewing vulnerable people and protecting their identities, it is imperative that you seek legal advice on how or whether that can be accomplished.

- Volunteer or freelance interviewers who refuse to relinquish work in progress if the oral history project disintegrates. Actually, if that happens, it's likely too late to prevent messy entanglements. That's why you should have volunteer or freelance interviewers—or anyone working for the project as an independent contractor—sign agreements at the outset making clear who has rights to the ownership and possession of the oral history materials in case the project ends before it's completed. Again, Neuenschwander's pamphlet offers a complete discussion of this issue.

ORAL HISTORY INTERVIEWING EQUIPMENT

While not a legal matter, myriad other considerations affect equipment selection for an oral history project, and chapter five provides complete details on the technological aspects of the many audio and video equipment choices available. But equipment choice and use also has an ethical dimension you should keep in mind as well. Here are some examples:

- While all recording equipment has a presence in the interview setting, video equipment in particular can be more intrusive than the equipment needed for an audio-only interview. Oral historians need to be sensitive to narrators' reluctance to appear on camera and respect their right to refuse to participate in a videotaped interview.

- Oral history projects that choose to videotape interviews also should make sure camera operators avoid unflattering camera angles and lighting that create harsh portrayals of narrators. While a videotaped oral history interview is not a documentary or a polished, rehearsed performance, it should not portray people negatively.

- Some oral historians argue that there is an ethical dimension to selecting recording equipment that fails to meet the test of time. As this manual makes clear, good oral history requires substantial planning and thorough research. To do that, and then have the interview materials themselves deteriorate rapidly or otherwise become unusable, is a disservice to everyone who participates in a project, but particularly to narrators whose time, energy, and memories made the project possible. Make every effort to maximize the quality of the equipment you choose, within the limits of your financial resources.

- Whatever the equipment choices, interviewers always should be thoroughly trained in its use. Failure to do so disrespects narra-

tors by wasting their time and resulting in a low-quality interview of limited usefulness.

- Videotaped interviews have greater potential for attracting interest from television production companies and other commercial interests, and narrators should be told that in the interest of fully informing them about the nature of the project.

PROJECT BUDGET

As chapter 6 describes, well-done oral history projects don't come cheaply, but creative project coordinators become adept at finding resources. Projects sponsored by companies and large institutions often are self-funded, while those sponsored by local, nonprofit, volunteer-run organizations often rely on funds from a wide variety of sources.

No matter what your sources of funds, always strive to maintain the intellectual integrity of the project and guard against any attempt by financial backers to control the content of the project or dictate topics or themes that must be pursued as a condition of funding. Publicity about the project, public exhibits or other materials developed as a result of the project, and permanent records of the collection, however, should include information about sources of funds or project sponsors.

INTERVIEW PREPARATION

The preparation required before an oral history interview is fundamental to its success, and, like the other steps in the oral history process, it has an ethical dimension.

Oral historians must conduct background research to the highest standards of scholarly integrity, taking care to document fully the sources of information consulted in the project's research phase. Providing such documentation makes it possible for future users of an oral history collection to put the interviews in context and understand the background against which the interviews took place.

The preparation phase, discussed in detail in chapter seven, is the point at which potential narrators are identified, and here, again, ethical issues arise. Narrators invited to participate in an oral history project should reflect the full range of perspectives about the topic or issue on which the oral history project focuses. This sometimes can be difficult precisely because oral history projects aim to find and collect previously undocumented accounts of often controversial events. But oral historians with a strong sense of ethics will commit themselves to creating as complete a historical contribution as possible.

THE INTERVIEW SETTING

As chapter 8 advises, practical considerations govern most of the decisions about where interviews take place. But just as equipment choices have an ethical dimension, so also do the choices about interview setting. While an oral history interview is not a relaxed social occasion, you can maximize the quality of an interview by assuring that it takes place where the narrator will be most comfortable. This is particularly important when narrators are elderly. Likewise, arrangements for the interview should not be unduly intrusive or disruptive, nor should they in any way exploit a narrator. Ethical oral historians, particularly in a videotaped oral history project, never should try to coax narrators into conducting their interviews in settings that would make them uncomfortable, no matter how visually interesting the settings might be.

THE INTERVIEW

Ethical conduct of the oral history interview is fundamental to the integrity of an oral history project. While chapter nine describes the process in detail, any discussion of oral history legal and ethical issues must stress the importance of respect for narrators and their stories as the underpinning of ethical interviewing. Interviewers show that respect by:

- adequate preparation and training that enables them to ask probing questions in a professional manner;
- familiarity with the equipment so they can operate it with confidence, thus assuring proper recording and preventing the equipment from becoming the focus of the interview;
- being sensitive to the diversity of their narrators and their perspectives and shunning thoughtless stereotypes that cloud understanding of people and issues;
- refraining from making promises that can't be fulfilled, such as guaranteeing that the oral history interview will be used or published;

- assuring that the narrator and interviewer properly sign the donor forms **at the conclusion of each interview session**. Some oral historians advocate summarizing the content of the form while the recorder is turned on—at either the beginning or end of the interview—and getting the narrator's verbal agreement with the terms of the document in addition to the concurrence in writing.

PROCESSING THE INTERVIEW

Processing and archival issues that relate to how the content of an oral history interview is to be made public raise a host of legal and ethical concerns.

If you plan for full transcriptions of the interviews, narrators customarily are permitted to review drafts of the transcripts to make corrections before the materials are made public. To streamline that process, but still maintain the ethical duty to allow narrators to review their transcripts, some oral history projects include in their release form a clause saying that the narrator has the right to review the transcript before it is put in final form. The document transfers copyright to the project, but commits the project to returning the transcript before making it public. Such release forms also often specify that if the narrator fails to return the transcript within a specified period of time—at least thirty days—it will be assumed that the transcript is correct and thus can become part of the oral history collection.

In addition to the copyright issue discussed earlier, another major legal issue comes into play in processing and archiving oral history materials. Make sure you have a procedure for reviewing the content of interviews to see if they contain potentially defamatory statements, which *Ballentine's Law Dictionary* defines as "anything which is injurious to the good name or reputation of another person, or which tends to bring him into disrepute." Defamatory statements can be spoken (slander) or written (libel).[2]

Neuenschwander's *Oral History and the Law* makes clear that oral history collections that include potentially defamatory statements made by narrators could be found equally guilty of defamation for disseminating such statements as the narrators who made the statements in the first place. While it's unclear just how frequently oral history narrators offer a slanderous remark, you need to be aware

> Oral history projects need to be aware of the potential legal pitfalls of disseminating potentially defamatory statements narrators might make. Generally words held to be defamatory relate to accusations of criminal, unethical, or immoral behavior, professional incompetence, financial irresponsibility, or association with despicable people.

of the possibility and need to be sure interviewers alert project coordinators whenever such statements occur in an interview. Generally, words held to be defamatory relate to accusations of criminal, unethical, or immoral behavior, professional incompetence, financial irresponsibility, or association with despicable people.

Established legal defenses against accusations of libel or slander fall into several categories. Among other points, they include:

- The person about whom the defamatory statement was made is dead; only the living can be libeled.

- The person about whom the defamatory statement was made is a public figure, not a private individual. While case law makes it much more difficult to libel a public official, the legal determination of just what constitutes a public or private figure often becomes the contentious part of a defamation claim.

- Truth is an absolute defense against charges of libel.

But rather than bank on the prospect of successfully defending a libel claim in court—likely an expensive prospect at best—many archives or repositories with oral history holdings rely on one of several options to protect themselves: editing out offending words in the transcript; masking the identity of the person about whom the libelous statement was made, or sealing offending portions of the interview. Again, sealing portions of an interview or closing it altogether for an extended period of time still would not protect the interview from being opened by court-ordered subpoena, which a narrator should be told.

ADDITIONAL OBSERVATIONS: ETHICS, ACCESS, AND MONEY

Some archivists and oral history project managers approach the collections management process with a strong conviction that access to the material should be controlled. They argue that researchers or others who want access to oral histories ought to be required to explain their purpose when seeking permission to use or quote from such materials. Attempts to assure that oral history materials are used only for purposes the repository deems responsible comes too close to censorship to make others comfortable. But concerns about censorship may take a back seat to the conviction that holders of oral history materials have an ethical obligation to assure that their narrators' words are not used in a way that makes them look foolish or misrepresents them. Some oral historians also believe that controlling use of oral histories is a safeguard to assure that the narrators whose words are used will not be exploited and that they will have a chance to benefit from possible commercial applications of oral history materials.

Commercial applications are, indeed, a reality for many kinds of museum and archival collections, as a host of film and television production companies increasingly turn to such collections for audio, video, and other materials for commercial purposes. Some nonprofit museums and archives, reluctant to be put in the position of subsidizing profit-making companies, have instituted sliding fee scales for use of such materials. Other repositories have contracts with marketing agencies that enable them to cash in on the value of photographs, interviews, or other elements of their collections for which there is a commercial demand. Such practices, while clearly beneficial to often poorly funded repositories, nonetheless raise questions about how to assure that the narrators themselves—or their heirs—also benefit from the commercial use of their words and voices.

While some project administrators or collections managers advocate controlling use of oral history materials, others see the Internet as a way to increase exponentially the number of users and ease of access to their materials. Many oral history projects have created Web sites that provide information about their collections, which poses little ethical concern. Others, however, have created Web sites with full-text transcripts of interviews, audio and video excerpts, and assorted other materials in the collection as well as links to related online resources. Such Internet access can be a researcher's dream, offering connections to collections that might be impossible to visit in person. The immediacy of voices and images online also can create a dramatic impact that captivates Web site visitors in ways that reading a transcript in an archives reading room cannot.

But ethical issues abound when oral history projects entertain the idea of creating a Web site as a product of the oral history process. Access to the Internet has become all but universal in the United States, thanks not only to the explosion in home computers but to the proliferation of computers and online services available through schools and public libraries. As a result, an oral history collection online is at least theoretically available to hundreds of millions of people, a far cry from the numbers that might visit and use a collection in a library or museum. That vast increase in the size of the potential audience makes it imperative that project coordinators who intend Internet distribution make sure narrators understand the scope of access on the World Wide Web. Many narrators might welcome the prospect; others might not.

Some oral historians worry that the narrator's knowledge that an interview is to be accessible to virtually anyone in the world who has access to a computer will affect the content of the interview itself. Will such widespread access lead narrators to engage in self-censorship to the point of blandness, where potentially valuable but controversial insights will be lost or never revealed? Or will the reverse happen, where narrators envisioning a cameo role on a global stage get carried away with their accounts?

If you decide to distribute interview materials online, be especially vigilant in reviewing materials for potentially defamatory language. Protecting against copyright violation also is more difficult with online materials. Oral history Web sites should contain copyright notices repeated both before and after the transcripts or excerpts, and audio and video or graphic materials can be protected from unauthorized use by putting them on the Internet in a less-than-broadcast-quality format.

Some oral history practitioners suggest another way out of the conundrum pitting the desire for universal access against the interest in protecting copyright for oral history projects: Renounce any copyright interest and assign the materials to the public domain, where all copyrighted materials end up eventually when the copyright terms expire. Pirating copyrighted materials from Web sites then would not be an issue, and anyone would be free to use the materials however they wanted. The disadvantage to such an approach, however, is that if someone used the materials for commercial purposes or misused them in the eyes of the narrator or the project's sponsors, the oral history creators would stand little chance of successfully seeking redress or claiming a share of any profits from their words.

While these legal and ethical concerns might seem to be enough to make would-be oral historians throw in the towel and look for an easier way to spend their energies, don't be discouraged. The legal and ethical framework in which oral historians work has evolved over more than half a century, and it has successfully guided the conduct of untold numbers of oral history interviews. While the rise of the Internet and other digital applications of oral history materials has introduced a new twist to the philosophical and ethical debates over the uses of oral histories, nothing has changed the fundamental ethical requirement that an oral history project be guided by intellectual integrity and a sense of respect for the men and women who are asked to share their stories.

Notes

1. John A. Neuenschwander, *Oral History and the Law*, 3d ed. (Carlisle: Oral History Association, 2002).

2. William S. Anderson, editor, *Ballentine's Law Dictionary*, 3d ed. (Rochester: The Lawyers Cooperative Publishing Company, 1969), 321.

CHAPTER 4

Getting Started

How do you develop a project and keep it organized? Oral history projects involve lots of people and lots of activity. Defining the initial structure and developing good organizational tools will make a big difference in how smoothly your project runs.

> **Initial Oral History Planning Steps**
>
> Select key leaders and project personnel
>
> Name the project
>
> Develop the mission statement
>
> Select a repository
>
> Decide on the equipment to use
>
> Develop a project budget
>
> Identify funding and support sources
>
> Select an advisory board
>
> Develop a timeframe for completing the project
>
> Develop record-keeping systems
>
> Develop a publicity plan
>
> Train the interviewers

SELECT KEY LEADERS AND PROJECT PERSONNEL

Oral history projects are labor intensive. As such, they offer opportunities for many people to be involved in various capacities. The first and most critical need is for a small group of leaders, the project planners or coordinators, who can make the time commitment to see the process through to its end. An oral history project resulting in fifteen to twenty interviews can take up to two years to complete. Project coordinators direct the project and determine its purpose, focus, budget, interview themes, number of interviews, and timeframe within which the work will be completed. Committed planners are essential to a project and often are the keys to success.

Oral history projects create sources of new information and new perspectives, but the work is time-consuming and can falter as participants move on to other interests. It helps to have several people take responsibility from beginning to end, and it often works best if one person agrees to serve as an overall project director to keep participants on task and the project in focus. Others should actively participate in the planning process. The group need not be large; in fact, a small group of no more than a half-dozen people is often most effective. The important factor is commitment to the project and willingness to take the lead in getting it done. These people may be paid or volunteer or both.

In addition to the project coordinators, oral history projects have other personnel needs. These usually include:

- interviewers,
- support staff, and
- transcribers.

Interviewers are the people who do the oral history interviews. Project coordinators also may be interviewers, but the work of the two should not be confused. Projects often start with an idea about people to interview and subjects to cover. Although people will be excited about doing the interviews, they should remember to keep this work in the context of the entire project. Applying the steps outlined in this manual will move the interviews from a scattershot collection of information to a cohesive oral history project.

Interviewers can expect to spend less time on the project than the coordinators do, but they should be able to give at least twenty to thirty hours per interview. This includes research and background preparation time, recording the interview, plus all scheduling and travel time involved and turning interview products over to the project director. This time commitment can be reduced somewhat if project coordinators do most of the work to develop the interview, but it will still take at least a fifteen- to twenty-hour commitment from the interviewer to insure solid preparation. The more complex the interview subject and themes, the more preparation time interviewers will need.

When choosing interviewers for the project, whether volunteer or paid, planners will want to look for people with specific characteristics. Good interviewers:

- are committed to the project;
- are willing to learn about the project topics and the specific information needed for an interview;
- are willing to attend all oral history training workshops and be screened for suitability as an interviewer or to fill some other project role (some would-be oral historians discover, for example, that they just can't stop talking long enough to listen to another person; such eager volunteers can be steered into one of the many other jobs that need to be done);
- have solid research and organizational skills;
- are willing to commit the necessary time to work on the project;
- listen carefully and thoroughly understand the need to let the narrator do the talking during the interview.
- are able to ask probing questions, to develop follow-up questions, and know when and how to ask them;
- can be flexible in scheduling time with narrators;
- exhibit good people skills, including the ability to draw out a narrator;
- are patient, tactful, and diplomatic and able to use these skills to keep an interview focused;
- exhibit respect for narrators and their stories, including being impartial to the subjects discussed and nonjudgmental toward the narrators;
- can control their own discomfort and manage their reactions in difficult or challenging situations;
- speak in a clear voice;
- practice using their equipment enough to be comfortable with it.

Although not all interviewers will possess all these skills, these are the types of interviewer characteristics that will be assets to the project.

You may be tempted to assume that journalists and others with interviewing experience automatically understand oral history. Often, however, they don't. While journalists and ethnographers, for example, ask questions and might record answers, the purposes for which they collect information differ from those of the oral historian in the types of questions asked, the ways in which the questions are asked, and the ways in which the information is used. Although people with other interviewing backgrounds can bring specific skills to an oral history project, they should be willing to learn about and adapt to the requirements of oral history interviewing.

In addition to interviewers, project support staff will vary, depending on your project's needs. A secretary or typist can be helpful if the project has money to hire someone or can find a volunteer. A person who is familiar with the equipment and can handle training and maintenance is also helpful.

Finding someone to transcribe the interviews is often a major hurdle for oral history project coordinators. Although many oral historians and users of the materials want ongoing access to the voices on the tape or disc, complete verbatim transcription is the best way to guarantee long-term access to the information in the interview, especially in this time of rapidly changing equipment and format types. Full transcription insures the information will remain accessible at least in written form. Characteristics of good transcribers (paid or volunteer) include:

- accurate typing skills;
- ability to operate (or learn to operate) the transcribing machines;
- ability to clearly hear electronic sound;
- ability to produce work on time and on schedule;
- a broad general background that lends itself to accurately hearing and typing the words spoken in the interview;
- the ability to translate the spoken word to the written page, including successfully determining paragraph and sentence structure, appropriate application of the rules of punctuation, and accurate spelling, while making a verbatim copy of the interview;
- high ethical standards, including an understanding to not discuss information in the interview.

If your project chooses not to transcribe the interviews, you will at least need to find someone to write an abstract or a log of the topics covered in the interview. This is also a time-consuming task, but results in a summary of the interview information rather than a verbatim transcript of the full interview. Some projects expect their interviewers to perform this task; if that's your plan, make sure your interviewers understand that at the outset.

Some oral history projects also include researchers. These people help with background research, developing and providing packets of information to project coordinators and interviewers. Their work can be very helpful if the planners and interviewers do not have time to do it themselves.

NAME YOUR PROJECT

Naming a project gives it an immediate identity. With this, it can begin to move forward. It also helps when looking for funding and developing stationery and other printed materials, and it creates a consistent identity in all your project publicity. This may be done before or after you write the mission statement.

WRITE YOUR PROJECT'S MISSION STATEMENT

Your project coordinator's first major task is to define the purpose of the project. This is done by developing a mission statement that specifically states the project's parameters. Your group will have many ideas about what information your oral history project should collect and the people to interview. A mission statement will help keep the project in focus and provide some realistic goals of what to accomplish.

The statement usually includes information on key areas of interest and importance for the project. It emphasizes that the work of the project will be to gather and preserve information that might otherwise be lost. It defines the time, place, and subject focus and states clearly what the project expects to include, but is flexible enough in its language to allow for adding important new directions that might evolve as the project progresses. Finally, it reaffirms the importance of conducting the work to the standards of the Oral History Association.

A mission statement need not be long. Several sentences incorporating the above points are usually sufficient. But developing this statement is not as easy as it sounds. It requires you to think carefully about the purpose of the project and to identify specifically what it will and will not include. Distilling this information into several concise sentences is a challenge, but it also helps you clarify the purpose of your work. Ultimately, the mission statement becomes the yardstick used to help decide who will and will not be interviewed when the number of potential narrators far outstrips your resources. See appendix 4 for a sample mission statement.

SELECT A REPOSITORY FOR THE MATERIALS YOUR PROJECT WILL CREATE

After you work through the above steps, your next major decision is choosing the organization or institution that will take ownership of all materials the project generates. If your project is already operating under the sponsorship of a library or museum, this is not an issue. But if that is not the case, finding a permanent home for your project materials is an important task. Suitable candidates for a permanent repository will depend on who is sponsoring the project and who has the appropriate facilities for storing materials and making them available to researchers. Libraries, museums, and other educational institutions are all likely candidates to consider. Each probably will have its own requirements for accepting collections, so you should make arrangements with the repository as early as possible in the project planning process.

You will want to make sure the materials you generate will be held by a repository that has the ability to safeguard the collection and make it as widely available as possible. When finished, the collection could include tapes or discs, video materials, transcripts or tape logs, and narrator files. And that may not be all. Many times, as a result of an interview, the narrator will offer the project historic photographs (which may either be copied and returned or kept, depending on the narrator's wishes), other archival materials, and related artifacts. When accepted, these also become part of the project collection and have the same need for ongoing care at the designated repository.

Look for a repository that will manage all project materials in accordance with the prevailing standards of the Oral History Association and professional archival administrators and curators. It should have written policies governing access to and care of its collections and should expect researchers who use its materials, including the oral history collections, to give the institution appropriate credit.

Always remember that the Internet is not a repository. While you can use it to disseminate information from the project, it should never be considered a permanent repository for storing project materials. It should also never be assumed that once materials are posted on the Internet, they will remain there permanently. Materials are lost when removed from the Internet unless other provisions have been made to save them.

If oral history project materials are not put in a standard repository, the chances of their being lost increase exponentially. Oral history projects that end up permanently stashed under someone's bed or in a closet or attic are as inaccessible to the general public as items lost from the Internet.

DECIDE ON THE EQUIPMENT YOU WILL USE

Detailed information on how to choose recording technology is included in chapter 5 of this manual. You will want to be aware of current recording standards and plan accordingly.

DEVELOP A PROJECT BUDGET

Even if your project will be staffed largely by volunteers, it will incur expenses. And while some of those may be met through volunteered time or donated materials, it is still important at the outset to determine realistically what funds will be required and when. A complete discussion of project costs is included in chapter 6.

IDENTIFY FUNDING SOURCES

Although chapter 6 will cover this in detail, be aware that even volunteer projects have costs that donated time and materials cannot cover. Funding sources can include outright grants, loans of equipment and other materials, and in-kind contributions. All may be necessary to successfully complete a project. The sooner you can identify possible support options, the faster and more smoothly your project can grow.

SELECT THE ADVISORY BOARD

The project advisory board is a group of people who can provide support for the project. This group should not be confused with the project planners or coordinators. The advisory board's purpose is to help find funding sources and additional support options, and to help with project needs such as legal advice when called upon to do so.

Advisory board members do not have to meet as a group or even meet regularly. Each may be called upon for a specific source of expertise and, thus, may offer help to the project at different times and in different ways. All, however, should be committed to the project and its goals and should thoroughly understand what their role is and why they have been asked to serve on the advisory board. Even if your advisory board does not meet regularly, you should keep board members informed with periodic reports about the progress of your project.

DEVELOP A TIME FRAME FOR COMPLETING THE PROJECT

Because oral history is time-consuming, a project time frame that establishes goals for completing project milestones—completing the research, preparing interview outlines, completing interviews—can be helpful.

Your project plan should allot time for:

- identifying interviewers and providing interviewer training;
- selecting narrators;
- continuing research, including narrator-specific work;
- scheduling and conducting interviews; and
- processing interviews.

Remember that oral history projects can change as new information is uncovered, so be prepared to remain flexible rather than slavishly adhering to your time frame.

CREATE YOUR RECORD-KEEPING SYSTEMS

After you reach an agreement with a project repository, you should develop record-keeping systems. A relatively invisible part of project development, this provides the continuity and support necessary for both interviewer and narrator. You don't want to get bogged down in paperwork, but developing five or six standard forms at the outset can help you keep track of the project while keeping the project on track.

Project forms are part of the interview support materials. Some of the most commonly used forms are listed below and illustrated here. Blank samples are in appendix 2. They include:

- donor (legal release) form,
- biographical information form,
- oral history interview information form,
- potential narrator information form,
- master log form, and
- artifact/archival information sheet.

The donor or legal release form, one of the most important records an oral history project will create, is discussed fully in chapter 3.

The biographical information form (fig. 4.1) contains basic biographical information about a narrator. Depending on how the project is organized, it may be filled out at the beginning of the interview or during a preliminary meeting or telephone conversation between the interviewer and narrator. It documents who the narrator is, both for project purposes and for the benefit of future researchers.

An oral history interview information form (fig. 4.2) is another important document. The interviewer should fill it out as soon as possible after an interview. It lists the names of the narrator and interviewer, the project name, interview date and length, and number of cassettes or discs, confirms that the donor form has been signed, and contains a one- to three-paragraph abstract or description of the substance of the interview. This form provides immediate access to the interview content even before full processing is completed. It also can contain pertinent information about the context of the interview and notes about interviewer or narrator that will provide facts useful to future users.

The potential narrator information form (fig. 4.3) is an important element of your record-keeping system for it helps you keep track of possible narrators. Project research will often uncover the names of people whose information could be important to the project, and additional names will surface as news about your project spreads. The potential narrator information form keeps up-to-date information about all such prospective narrators including full names, home and work addresses, home and work telephone and fax numbers, and other contact information, such as e-mail addresses. It also should include a brief summary of each person's background and information he or she can contribute to the project.

Other suggested forms are the master log form (fig. 4.4) and archival and artifact inventory form (fig. 4.5). The master log form identifies all contacts with narrators. It shows the status of each interview, its length, and processing status, and provides a capsule summary of project progress at any point in time.

The archival and artifact inventory form lists additional materials the narrator might give an interviewer during the interview. Oral history interviews are generally done in a narrator's home or other community location, and interviewers often learn about additional information, including photographs, memorabilia, and other materials that narrators sometimes wish to give to the project repository, too. An inventory form can help keep track of these archival materials, identifying them and their donors. A columnar form is easy to use—one column identifies the item, a second provides a place for a description, and a third indicates suggested disposition (e.g., "given as a gift," "would like copies made and returned"). The interviewer signs the form and keeps it with the materials to be turned over to the repository.

If a copy cannot be given to the narrator at the time, the interviewer should make one and send it to him or her as quickly as possible. It helps if the interviewer stays involved in this process until the materials are returned or donated, checking with the repository to clarify any questions about their disposition and with the narrator to clarify any questions about the process.

Finally, project coordinators are responsible for keeping the project files, including a master file for each narrator and separate files containing research materials and other project background information.

The master file, which should remain confidential, usually contains:

- the full name, home and work addresses, telephone and fax numbers, and e-mail address of the narrator,
- all correspondence with the narrator,
- notes from conversations with the narrator, whether by telephone or in person,
- the biographical information form,
- potential narrator information form,
- the completed interview information form,
- the original copy of the signed donor form,
- the interview outline,
- narrator-specific research materials,

- interview notes,
- lists of people and place names mentioned during the interview with the narrator's spelling corrections,
- a black-and-white photograph of the narrator in the interview setting,
- a more formal photo given by the narrator, if desired, and
- a draft of the transcript containing the narrator's comments and corrections.

Setting up an organized records system at the beginning of the project will save much time and frustration as the project develops. It will also help ensure all necessary materials can be accounted for.

DEVELOP A PUBLICITY PLAN

Be sure to give some thought to creating a project publicity plan. This is an essential, but often overlooked, element of any successful oral history project. The oral history interviews, when completed, will represent an important addition of new information or new perspectives, and publicizing the collection's existence should not be neglected.

At the outset of your project, a publicity plan might include printing a brochure describing the project and giving the names of coordinators and supporters. This can be an excellent piece both for the general public and to give to prospective narrators. You also could design and print stationery to use on all project correspondence as a way to reinforce your project's public identity.

Sometimes project coordinators think it will help generate good publicity if they issue a press release asking for would-be narrators to step forward. Resist the temptation to do that unless you've found absolutely no other way to identify potential narrators. A public request for narrators implies a promise to interview anyone who comes forth, which may not be in the best interests of your project. The choice of narrators is better made through careful research.

Although some work on the publicity plan will take place at the beginning of the project, most will occur after the information has been collected and the project is complete. At this time, you will want to announce project results to the general public. Send brief press releases to all local news media and other organizations—local, state, national, or international—that might have an interest in the information you've collected.

TRAIN YOUR INTERVIEWERS

The ideal situation is to find trained oral history interviewers who are familiar with a project's subject. Since this is rarely possible, you should arrange for interviewer training sessions and project orientation sessions as part of the planning and development process. This is essential to creating good oral history interviews.

An orientation and training workshop should include discussion of your project's goals as well as general background about the oral history process. Would-be interviewers, no matter how much other interviewing experience they might have as journalists, ethnographers, social scientists, or human resources personnel, *all* need to learn about the unique characteristics of the oral history interview. The Oral History Association annual fall meetings always include a variety of informative workshops for beginning and advanced oral history practitioners, and state or regional oral history organizations around the nation schedule workshops throughout the year. See chapter 12 for information on reaching these sources.

In addition, state historical societies, state or regional museums associations, local colleges and universities, and state humanities councils can be resources for oral history training. Experienced oral historians often are available to create workshops customized to meet your needs. Indeed, some projects schedule several training sessions, one at the beginning of a project and a subsequent session after interviewers have had a chance to complete one or two interviews and have their work critiqued. As new interviewers join a project team, training should always be offered. Haphazard or insufficient training is certain to be a project's downfall. Even the best-planned oral history projects can fizzle if interviewers lack the skills they need to get started or to improve their work once the interviewing phase is under way.

This initial planning for organizing and coordinating your work, while a time-consuming task, lays the groundwork for a solid, well-executed oral history project. Through this process, you will define the focus and direction of the project and provide a sound basis for collecting historical information.

BIOGRAPHICAL INFORMATION FORM

Name _Jane Doe_

Address(home) _456 Smith Lane_
Amarillo, Texas

Address(work) _24679 Post Road_
Amarillo, Texas

Telephone (home) _42-724-9675_ Telephone (work) _42-727-1234_ E-mail _jd@adr.net_

Birth Date and Year _9/27/42_

Birth Place _Houston, Texas_

Profession _teacher_

Spouse or Closest Living Relative _John Doe_

Maiden Name (if applicable) _Smith_

Biographical Information (please include the names of parents, siblings, spouse, and children if applicable to the oral history interview):

John + Joan Smith – parents
James + Janie Doe – children
B.A. in English 1963
M.A. in Education 1967

Date _10/29/01_

Form Filled Out By _J D_

Figure 4.1. An example of a filled-out Biographical Information Form.

INTERVIEW INFORMATION FORM

Name _John Doe_

Address _429 1st Street_
Enid, Oklahoma

Interviewer _____

Date of Interview _October 16, 1989_

Place of Interview _Mr. Doe's home_

Length of Interview _1.7 hours_

Number of Cassettes or Discs _two_

Oral History Donor Form Signed _10/16/89_ (Date)
Unrestricted _X_
Restricted ____

Transcript Reviewed by Narrator _12/20/89_ (Date)

Abstract of Interview:

Mr. Doe described his World War II memories, beginning with where he was on December 7, 1941, and then recounting his induction into the Army after he finished high school. He spoke, for the first time, of his experiences during the Battle of the Bulge and of being captured and sent to a prisoner of war camp during this battle. Finally, he described the end of the war and coming home.

Figure 4.2. An example of a filled-out Interview Information Form.

POTENTIAL NARRATOR INFORMATION FORM

Name _Jane Doe_

Address _123 Sweetbriar Lane_

Philadelphia, Pennsylvania

Telephone(home) _212-523-1234_ Telephone(work) _212-578-6789_

E-mail _jd @ abd.net_   Fax _212-567-2345_

Potential Narrator File Information:

_Ms. Doe was an eyewitness to
the event we are documenting. She
is interested in our project and
is willing to discuss her memories.
She works during the day, but
has time in the evenings and on
weekends to be interviewed._

Form Filled Out By _abc_

Date _10/20/01_

Figure 4.3. An example of a filled-out Potential Narrator Information Form.

PROJECT MASTER LOG

Narrator	Interviewer	Interview Date	Release Signed (note type)	Draft Transcript to Narrator	Processing Done (note type and by whom)	Artifacts/ Photos (cross reference to form)	Put in Repository
John Doe	Mary Smith	9/10/98	9/10/98	11/2/98	3/20/99 Transcript by AR	Yes see form	4/1/99
James Doe	Mary Smith	11/20/98	11/20/98 Restricted	12/15/98		NA	
Jane Doe	Mary Smith	1/25/99	1/25/99	2/20/99	3/17/99 Tape log by AR	NA	4/1/99
Julie Doe	Mary Smith	2/10/99	2/10/99			Yes see form	

Figure 4.4. An example of a filled-out Master Log Form.

ARTIFACT AND ARCHIVAL INVENTORY FORM

Name _John Doe_

Address _123 Anderson Lane_
Butte, Montana 58123

Item	Description	Status
1. photo of copper mining	1950-55 Berkeley Pit	on loan, please copy and return
2. copper miners	Summer, 1954 at Berkeley Pit l-r: Doe, Anton Peterson, James Peterson, James Doe, unknown	on loan, please copy and return
3. hard hat	1950's, used in Berkeley Pit	gift, please send donor form

Figure 4.5. An example of a filled-out Artifact and Archival Inventory Form.

CHAPTER 5

Recording Technology

What equipment should you use? Oral historians have faced this question since the research technique evolved during World War II. This chapter will provide information about the characteristics of specific equipment types. The following chapters will deal with costs and the impact of equipment choices on an interview.

The information presented here might seem complex and you might wonder how much you really need to know. Misinformation or confusion about equipment basics, however, can stall a project or, even worse, result in losing all the information so carefully collected. For instance, unknowingly using a proprietary digital format (one that can be used only with permission from the owner and is subject to arbitrary change or loss) when recording the interview will likely cause loss in the long run. Some oral history projects have found this out the hard way.

Although this sounds intimidating, it isn't written to alarm you. We hope, instead, that by presenting the following information we will help you avoid as many equipment pitfalls as possible in this rapidly changing technological environment.

A BRIEF HISTORY OF RECORDING EQUIPMENT

Ethnologists and folklorists were the first to use equipment to make field recordings.[1] Beginning in the 1890s, ethnologists began recording the music of Native Americans using wax cylinders or discs (hard wax surfaces into which sound grooves were cut). Others used the equipment to record folk music (fig. 5.1).

Recording technologies that would give rise to oral history began with the invention of the tape recorder, a machine that takes electric current representing sound from a microphone and passes it over an electromagnet or "record head," which magnetizes the iron oxide coating on a ribbon or "tape," commonly made of acetate but more recently of Mylar, as it moves past the head. This captures the sound so it can be preserved and reproduced at a later time. Most recorders have one or two additional heads. The playback head, which may be the same as the record head, replays the information on the tape. The erase head scrambles

information, giving the record head a clean tape to work with. The first such recorder was called a Magnetophone and was developed in Germany between World War I and World War II. The wire recorder, which used steel tape or wire as the recording medium, was developed in the United States in 1939. Although not marketed to the general public until after World War II, this equipment eventually led to mass availability of recording equipment that was more reliable and portable than anything previously available.[2]

The availability of wire recorders led to the development of the first oral history programs. In 1944, Sgt. Forrest Pogue of the U.S. Army's Historical Division used them to record accounts of the D-Day invasion.[3] Shortly after World War II, Allan Nevins of Columbia University used them on an oral history project collecting information about prominent New Yorkers. The work of Pogue and Nevins helped establish the oral history field and the use of the oral history archive to collect and maintain information gathered during interviews.

Others quickly built on their work, including historians at the Bancroft Library at the University of California, Berkeley, and in the U.S. Army. Interest spread and many scholars recognized oral history as an interesting new field through which recorded interviews could be used to gather and preserve information from all kinds of people about a wide range of topics. Questions about the type of equipment to use, however, surfaced almost immediately. Wire recorders, while a great improvement over the field equipment folklorists and ethnologists used before World War II, were still bulky and prone to breakdowns.

Interest in magnetic recording in the United States began with tape coating experiments at Minnesota Mining and Manufacturing (3M Company) in 1944. Discovery of several Magnetophones in Frankfurt, Germany, near the end of World War II furthered the work. These analog machines (referring to recorders that capture data through a "continuously fluctuating flow of current analogous to the data it represents"),[4] were brought back to the United States and demonstrated to broadcasters at the San Francisco Institute of Radio Engineers in

Figure 5.1. Omaha Indian, Good Old Man, singing into a phonograph in 1905. The photograph was taken by ethnologist Marvin Gilmore. *Photo credit: A.E. Sheldon Lantern Slide Collection. RG2039-100. Nebraska State Historical Society.*

1946. Ampex successfully developed a U.S.-made magnetic recorder and, in 1948, one of these machines and 3M acetate audiotape on an open reel was used to record a live Bing Crosby radio show in New York for broadcast several hours later on the West Coast.

Known as reel-to-reel recorders because the blank tape (supply) was on an open reel and was threaded to move past the "head" to a take-up reel, these machines began to replace wire recorders as the industry standard.[5] Although the reel-to-reel format remained in common use until the mid-1960s and is still considered the archival standard for preserving sound, industry advancements led to the portable, self-contained tape recorder in 1951. Audio cassettes (audiotape housed in plastic cases containing both the supply and take-up reels) were first developed and put on the market in 1963, and Sony later introduced portable audio cassette players (fig. 5.2).

Digital technology (referring to the use of "discrete numerical values that represent data" and are read by a computer)[6] began to make an impact in the 1990s with growing interest in compact discs (CDs—optically read discs originally containing digitally encoded information) and CD players, followed by Compact Discs Read Only Memory (CD-ROMs—optically read discs on which memory storage is encoded).[7] Digital Audio Tape (DATs—magnetic tapes formatted to record and play back digital audio) players and minidiscs (smaller CDs and CD-ROMs) and minidisc players began to come into common usage during that time as well.

Developments in video recording technology have moved as fast as the audio recording field. Ampex began work on videotape (magnetic tape used to capture moving pictures and synchronized sound for preservation and later reproduction) and a videotape recorder (VTR) in 1951. The first home VTR was marketed in 1963. The first videocassette (videotape housed in a plastic case), the 3/4-inch U-Matic one-hour tape, was introduced in 1969 and became the world standard for videocassettes at the time.

Videocassette recorders (VCRs) were introduced in the early 1970s, ushering in what became known as the "Betamax Battles," with Beta and VHS (video home system) formats vying for market supremacy. Beta offered superior resolution, but was surpassed in popularity by VHS systems. Beta evolved into the professional Beta-Cam format, which supplanted the 3/4-inch U-Matic cassette.

The first consumer video camcorder (portable videotaping equipment—its name is a contraction of camera and recorder) was introduced by Sony in 1980 for use with VHS and (in 1985) 8-mm formats. The 1980s saw the introduction of a variety of types of videotape, including Beta HiFi VCR, and the Hi-8, S-VHS, and VHS-C (higher-resolution) formats for VHS. Each had specific attributes—some had good sound quality but poor picture quality, others had good picture quality but poor sound. Others had length limitations. The VHS-C, for example, had only a 20-minute recording capacity.

The introduction of digital video (a "video signal represented by binary digits that describe a set of colors and luminance levels" that is converted by computer to moving pictures)[8] formats brought additional variety to the market. The major product was the DVD (Digital Versatile Disc, also known as Digital Video Disc—a double-sided compact disc), for which commercial standards were agreed to in 1995.

HOW DOES YOUR CHOICE OF EQUIPMENT FIT INTO THE ORAL HISTORY PLANNING PROCESS?

As you can see from this brief overview of the evolution of various recording formats, the one constant in recording history is change. Formats are created and abandoned, and at any one time many different formats are available from which to choose. Oral historians can easily become bewildered by the range of equipment options.

Few discussions result in such heated exchanges of ideas among oral historians as those involving the pros and cons of different equipment types. Advice from prominent leaders in the field ranges from those who say to work only in analog to those who advise oral historians to throw out analog and use only digital. Understanding the range of equipment types, how they work, and what they produce, will help you make the best decision for your project.

This doesn't mean all oral historians must be experts in recording technology or the interviews will be lost. But a working knowledge of the basics can make the difference between success and failure. Depending on your level of interest or expertise, you may want to enlist help at this point in your project from a person with a strong background in computers and recording technology, such as radio or television station personnel or a middle or high school teacher. It is important to remember that

Figure 5.2. Recorder and media examples, including a reel-to-reel tape, a wire recorder, a wax cylinder, an analog recorder, a dictation disc, a compact disc, a tape cassette, a wire recording, a "45," and a transcription disc. This a small example of the type of equipment and media an archives might contain. *Photo credit: Barbara W. Sommer.*

anyone you look to for advice should understand, or be willing to learn about, the specific recording needs of oral history, especially the need for continuing access to the full interview as spoken and maximizing longevity of the original recording.

Decisions about the type of equipment to use, thus, are central to the planning process. The choice of equipment affects, and is affected by, all other decisions you make. These include: cost, availability and use policies for existing equipment, project goals, collecting policies of possible project repositories, availability of interviewer training, ease of use in the interview setting, purpose of the interview, impact on the narrator, and long-term accessibility and longevity of the materials.

Before analyzing the characteristics of each of the recording equipment devices, you should talk to the manager of the repository where your collection ultimately will reside. Most repositories, whether small volunteer-run or large, multi-faceted organizations, have standards for what they will and will not accept. Working with the archivist or person in charge of accepting materials can save you much time and expense. They can help you understand the specific institutional criteria, including equipment-related issues. Be sure to ask about sound and image quality standards, analog and digital formats, and any format requirements you should meet.

The purpose of this chapter is neither to recommend one type of equipment or another nor to recommend specific brands or models. It is, rather, to give you the background to make the most beneficial choices from the variety available for your project. And it is to help you remember, as James E. Fogerty, director of the Minnesota Historical Society's oral history program, recently wrote, to keep "technology [as] a tool and not a controlling force" in a project.[9]

The basic equipment questions you will want to answer in planning an oral history project are:

- Should you use audio or video or a combination of the two?
- Should you use analog or digital?
- What should you know about the types of equipment on the market?
- What should you know about the tapes or discs, also called the media, used to record sound and images?
- What should you know about continuing accessibility?

- What should you know about tape, disc, software, hardware, and equipment longevity?

These questions are discussed here.

SHOULD YOU USE AUDIO OR VIDEO OR A COMBINATION OF THE TWO?

This is the first recording technology question you will face. Your decision will be based on the project budget, the purposes for doing the project, planned uses of the interviews, type and availability of long-term care of the final product, and narrator preferences. Each of these factors is important. Because video combines audio recording with visual images, it is also a more complex medium than audio alone and requires more planning. Depending on the type of video used, you will want to be aware of factors such as the intrusiveness of extra lights, equipment, and personnel and the possible resulting impact on interviewer-narrator interaction. Video equipment should be used by someone trained to handle the added technical elements that are part of a successful video production. This can mean involving professional operators or videographers, an added expense. Project directors sometimes expect the interviewer to operate the camera. Care should be taken, for each job requires full-time concentration to make the most of the interview situation. An experienced interviewer may find using a digital video camera allows one person to film while conducting an interview, but this should be done by someone

Audio and Video

Audio
Can be less costly
More flexibility in interview setting
Depending on the type of equipment, may allow for stronger interviewer-interviewee bonding
Can be less intrusive

Video
Can be more costly
Depending on type of equipment, can involve additional personnel
More complex interview setting needs
Provides access to visual materials

knowledgeable about interviewing and trained in this process. If you don't have access to trained personnel in your project, a professional camera operator can provide expertise, including knowledge of types of equipment, lenses, lighting, sound, interview setting, longevity of the video itself, and the additional technical details that affect the quality of the final product.

Sometimes video is necessary. Interviews done in sign language are a good example of this. Video interviews also document other nonverbal communications, such as gestures, facial expressions, and body language, and "expressions that are too complex or subtle to reduce to words"[10] and, as such, collect information that cannot be communicated in an audio interview. Although most oral history interviews are conducted one-on-one, video is useful if an interview involves more than one narrator since it makes it easier to see who is saying what. It is also useful if the narrator has items to show that visually enhance the interview. Video also can provide material for possible exhibit or Internet uses, although, as with all the above situations, development of useful footage involves careful planning.

There are options for combining audio and video. First, recording an audio interview and then working with the narrator to record visual images that supplement or complement it can be very effective. This allows projects to include video recording techniques while not relying exclusively on them. For example, thirty-two narrators were recorded through the Minnesota Historical Society's Minnesota Environmental Issues Oral History Project. After completing these interviews, project director James E. Fogerty followed up with video interviews with four narrators, each at a location that illustrated information given during the narrator's audio interview. Through careful planning for the video in a follow-up interview, Fogerty was able to gather additional information in a setting that maximized the use of visual images.

SHOULD YOU USE ANALOG OR DIGITAL EQUIPMENT?

Simply put, the difference in these machines is in the way they record sound and images. Both types of equipment transform sound and images into electrical current, which is then stored on a tape or a disc. Analog audio machines use magnetic tape to record sound. It is saved in a continuous pattern as it is heard; in other words, the signal recorded on the tape is a direct analog to the sound itself. Digital audio machines use either digital audiotapes or compact discs to capture the sound. Rather than record sound as it is heard, digital machines use various software programs and hardware to record sound as an average, taking samples of the signal and mathematically balancing it, then storing it on the tapes or discs as bits of data the way a computer stores information.

Digital machines are able to record and store large amounts of information by compressing the data into more compact forms, discarding anything they identify as redundant. Access to the compacted materials comes through a CODEC (a compression-decompression algorithm that processes digital files) that works with the specific software and hardware. CODECs vary, depending on the desired use of the audio or moving image file.

Archivists recognize analog reel-to-reel magnetic tape as the most stable medium and as the archival standard for sound recordings because it is thicker than other types of magnetic tape and holds sound better, it is not compressed, and sound on it is retrievable through universal, accessible equipment.

Analog and Digital

Analog
Does not need software or hardware to access
Sound and video are exact representations
Is not compressed
If tapes deteriorate, information is usually retrievable
Archival standard for sound and video recordings
Can be easily transferred to digital

Digital
Sound is more even
Recorders often require less maintenance
Tapes and discs hold more information
Copies may be made without degradation in many cases
Can be more easily edited; helpful for programming or Internet use
Requires use of specific software and hardware formats, which change frequently
If tapes or discs deteriorate, information is more difficult or impossible to retrieve

Its use, however, is decreasing because of the cumbersome nature of the equipment compared to the more compact cassette and digital recorders, difficulty in finding tape stock, and the erroneously perceived inferiority of its quality. If you decide to use analog recorders, it will probably be with audiocassettes. The most-often recommended type for oral historians is the 60-minute type II (high voice quality) normal or high bias analog cassette.

Analog and digital each have advantages and disadvantages, which are summarized in the accompanying sidebar. Briefly, the advantages of analog are: universal equipment, lack of compression, less complex format, relative ease of repairing media, and ease of transferring to digital as needed. Disadvantages include lower signal-to-noise ratio (relationship between the strength of the signal compared to unwanted noise) and loss of quality with each duplication (dub or copy). The advantages of digital include: more even sound, media (tapes or discs) that hold more information, ability to make clones (copies) without loss of quality on some types of media, and ease of editing or formatting for program use. Disadvantages include reliance for both use and retrievability on software and hardware formats that change frequently and difficulty or impossibility of repairing damaged media which can result in loss of information. Many projects use a combination of analog and digital, keeping copies in analog for archival purposes while using digital for public access and programming.

If you plan to use video recording equipment, you also will have to choose between analog and digital. The differences in the recording processes for video are similar to those for audio described above. Images are translated into electronic signals, which are then handled either in analog or digital format. Analog captures sound and image as it is presented, while digital records a mathematically balanced average, which it then stores on the tape or disc as bits of data using discrete numerical values to represent the information.

As with audio, digital video equipment can record and store large amounts of material by compressing the information (reducing the data representing the sequence of images). This is done by encoding (translating sound and images into digital format) differences between frames and discarding similarities.

The archival format for video is analog—specifically Betacam-SP—for reasons similar to those for sound recordings. As with audio, projects can consider combining analog and digital, keeping the analog for archival purposes while using the digital for ease of editing and program development.

Many oral historians run an audio back-up during a video interview. Another alternative is to make a copy of the audio from the video interview. Although not capturing the nuances of nonverbal communication, this copy provides a back-up of the interview and can be more easily used in transcribing. This is often done in analog as a back-up archival copy.

Whether using audio or video, the interviewer should take a still photograph of the narrator in the interview setting. This becomes part of the master file and is kept as a permanent visual record of the interview. Questions about use of digital are relevant for this part of the process, too. A digital camera will give you images you can transfer to a computer or a Web site, but, just as digital recorders compress sound and video, they compress images and thus contain less information than film. Photographs taken with digital cameras often pixelate (disintegrate into the individual squares that comprise them) when enlarged and are not currently designed to be saved for future generations. To take photos that will have longevity, use 35mm film. For photos that will last many generations, archivists recommend using black-and-white film processed to archival standards, such as using long-lasting paper and developing by hand in a darkroom. Your state archives will have the most up-to-date information on current processing and storage standards.

The decisions to use analog or digital, and audio or video or some combination, are important because they have a long-term impact on the development and continued use of project materials. The remaining sections of this chapter will focus on recording technology and its impact on: the interview, the accessibility of interview information, and the longevity of the tapes and discs used to record the information.

WHAT SHOULD YOU KNOW ABOUT THE TYPES OF EQUIPMENT ON THE MARKET AND THEIR IMPACT ON THE INTERVIEW?

The most important issue for oral historians to consider is quality of the final product. The best way to achieve optimum quality is with broadcast-quality recording equipment and media (tapes or discs). Broadcast quality refers to analog standards for radio and to analog and digital standards for television. Specifications are defined by the National Television Standards Committee (NTSC) of the Federal Communications Commission for the level of quality at which radio or television stations will transmit. Digital standards for television were adopted in 1996 and stations were given ten years to comply. Information on digital television standards may be obtained from the Advanced Television Systems Committee (ATSC). The American National Standards Institute (ANSI) is also a good source of information about standards. Specifications for broadcast quality change periodically. In addition to the above agencies, audio-visual archivists, local television and radio stations, and the Oral History Association are some good sources for the most up-to-date information available (fig. 5.3).

Your oral history project probably will not need equipment made for high-quality music recording, but you should maximize the life and use of the interviews with the best voice and/or visual-quality recording machines you can acquire. Typically, recorders manufactured for home use, while perhaps sounding good at the time of the initial recording, rarely meet broadcast-quality standards. If you are using analog recording formats, avoid mini-cassettes. Not only do they not meet broadcast-quality standards, they are especially prone to damage if mishandled. Also avoid voice-activated tape recorders. They shut down when people aren't talking, omitting pauses in the interview that can be important to understanding its context. Each stop and start also inserts a breaking sound on the tape that mars overall quality.

Never use the built-in microphone on the recorder. Instead opt for an external microphone to maximize quality. An external microphone is more sensitive and allows future listeners to clearly hear the interviewer and the narrator (that is, the full structure of the interview) without the distraction of motor noise from the recorder. As with the recorder, this should be a broadcast-quality piece of equipment. Make sure it is insulated to prevent picking up extra noise when touched. It can be an omnidirectional microphone (one that picks up all voices in a field around it), a cardiod microphone (one that picks up sound in a field around the source with less background noise), or a lavaliere (clip-on) microphone. Projects using clip-ons will need to have individual microphones for each person in the interview with corresponding connections to the recorder.

You will want to know if your recorder is monophonic or stereophonic. Stereo systems have the option of recording the sound on two channels—left and right, while monophonic has only one channel and one microphone jack. If you are using a microphone requiring a stand or pad, you will also want to consider whether to use a condenser or a dynamic. A condenser translates acoustical signals into electrical ones using a variable capacitor (a voltage-storing component), which requires a battery. A dynamic translates acoustical signals into electrical ones using a coil moving in a magnetic field. It generates its own electrical current and, thus, does not need a battery.

Equipment accessories also are important. Headphones permit the interviewer to monitor sound while the interview is in progress and resolve any audio problems that develop. Cables and connectors between the microphone and recording equipment are shielded (the conductors in them are wrapped) to reduce interference. Coaxial cables (with inner and outer conductors) are used for video recording. Cables should also be broadcast-quality. Even with the best equipment and microphones, the quality of sound and visual recording will be compromised with poor quality cables. Sturdy, stable microphone stands are also essential. These vary from free-standing models to those that clamp onto a flat surface to soft foam pads made especially to hold a microphone. Both cables and stand should allow for maximum flexibility in positioning the recorder and microphone.

There is also specialized equipment for recording over the telephone. Through use of a special attachment between telephone and recorder, you can conduct an audio interview over the phone. Several types of attachments are available, and project coordinators will want to use those that produce broadcast-quality sound.

WHAT SHOULD YOU KNOW ABOUT THE TAPES OR DISCS THAT RECORD THE SOUND OR VIDEO?

Another factor in choosing equipment is the specific type of media (tapes or discs) each uses. Options range from reel-to-reel analog magnetic tape to DVDs. As with types of recording equipment,

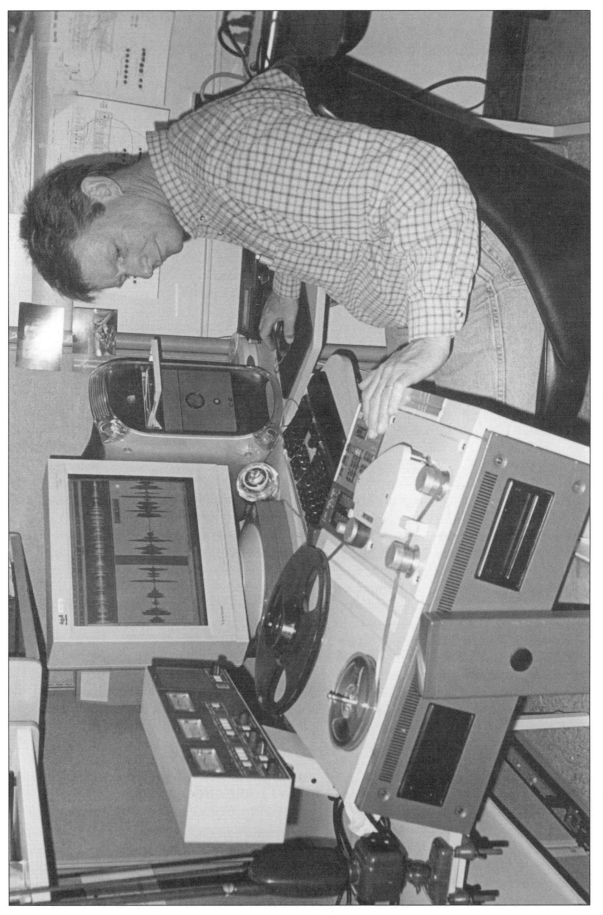

Figure 5.3. Nebraska State Historical Society audio-visual archivist Paul J. Eisloeffel with some of the tools that can be used for working with oral history recordings. *Photo credit: Barbara W. Sommer.*

each medium has specific characteristics. Analog recording machines use magnetic tape (a thin, inelastic strip of material coated with ferromagnetic emulsion) stored either on an open reel or in a plastic case (cassette). Sound is recorded on the tape as it is heard. The copy made during the interview is the master or original. Copies of the master, called dubs, are counted as generations, and each generation removed from the master declines or degrades in overall quality. While audio tapes generally work well and have a proven track record, bleed-through of voices from one layer of tape to another can occur if they are not taken out and played (sound on or sound off) at least once a year. They are also vulnerable to hydrolysis, which causes the tape to become sticky and to shed when played back. Broken or torn tapes may be spliced together with little loss of information.

Magnetic tapes may also be formatted to store digital data. These are called digital audiotapes (DATs). In addition to the sound, DATs record track number and time code calculated from the beginning of the tape. Up to 120 minutes may be recorded on a single tape and duplicates (sometimes called clones) can be made with little degradation.

Other types of digital equipment record onto compact discs. Compact discs are plastic-coated, optically read discs. Some are compressed; those using WAV (waveform sound files, identified by the .wav extension) are regarded as uncompressed, although software and hardware are still needed to read them because they are digital. Minidiscs, another recording medium, are smaller discs and are compressed. As with DAT, they have a time strip facilitating access. Both CDs and minidiscs are relatively stable mediums, but if the plastic coating (which holds the information) comes loose, you run the risk of losing all information. They are also vulnerable to heat and fingerprints and poor care can result in irreparable damage. Although copies of some digital materials can be made with no loss of quality, if the information is compressed, repeated copying can result in some loss of information. Changing technologies (software and hardware) affect continued availability of playback equipment for both CDs and minidiscs. As mentioned above, the choice for analog is the 60-minute high voice quality analog cassette. The choice for digital is an uncompressed compact disc.

Media are also a factor in the choice of video equipment. Videotape is a type of magnetic tape that records synchronized audio and video tracks. Analog videotape standards are defined by tape widths, with the larger widths indicative of higher quality recordings. Betacam-SP, the archival video format, is a stable, broadcast-quality 0.5-inch tape. Other types, especially S-VHS and Hi-8 (enhanced 8mm), although popular consumer items that produce a good product, do not meet broadcast-quality standards. Hand-held video cameras and low-end VHS video manufactured for home use are never recommended for oral history use. They do not record to broadcast-quality standards and the long-term viability of the product is unproven at best.

Magnetic videotapes are also developed for digital use. They are generally in formats such as DV, which have been developed for the consumer market. Formats such as D-1, D-2, and D-5 are used commercially and can be very expensive. Digital videotapes can allow multiple copies (clones) to be dubbed without loss of quality over generations.

Some digital equipment uses discs rather than magnetic tape. CDs and DVDs are optically read discs with multiple layers that can hold any type of digital data, including video and audio. A DVD holds more information than a CD because it compresses data more densely.

As stated above, CODECs process compressed audio and video digital signals. Some of the more widely known CODECs are MP3, CinePak, and Sorenson. Their uses vary depending on whether they are processing still photos, audio, or video. Each, however, has a compression ratio (the size of the original uncompressed data file divided by the size of its compressed version) that expresses the degree to which compression has occurred. Although this process normally runs smoothly, it is important to know that with too much compression or an incorrect ratio, artifacts (sounds or images that shouldn't be there) can appear and, if they do, they can permanently affect the quality of the digitized materials. You will also want to ask about the effects of compression on multiple copies made over time.

WHAT ARE THE TECHNICAL CHARACTERISTICS AND WHAT OTHER QUESTIONS SHOULD YOU ASK TO MAKE GOOD DECISIONS ABOUT RECORDING DEVICES FOR YOUR PROJECT?

What features does the equipment have and which will be the most useful for your project? For interview needs, these will include sound quality, ease of use of the equipment, and ongoing availability of equipment, tapes or discs, and accessories.

What is your project budget? Equipment costs are high and will be a factor in developing any project. Given the goal of using broadcast-quality equipment, what can your project realistically afford? This figure should also include the costs of tapes or discs. Whether working in analog or digital, audio or video, you'll need to keep a preservation master (the original recording) of the interview, and should add the costs of buying extra tapes or discs to make processing or user copies, copies for the narrator and audio back-up if using video. Finally, the availability of equipment to copy the tapes or discs is a factor to consider.

Who will be doing the interviewing and who will train interviewers to use the equipment? Thorough interviewer training on recording equipment is essential. Nothing is worse than sending someone out on an interview, only to find inexperience with the equipment results in either a poor quality product or complete loss of the information. Inexperienced or untrained interviewers also may pay more attention to the equipment than to the narrator, which can lower the quality of the interview.

Who is available for help if needed? Interviewer training does not completely solve the equipment use issue. Whether using volunteers, graduate assistants, or interviewers with many years' experience, there are times when it is helpful to have someone to turn to with questions about use of the equipment. Knowing your community and the kinds of expertise available for various types of recording equipment can help you choose equipment best suited to your needs.

What are the interviewing conditions? Conditions at the interview setting can affect your equipment decisions. What are the conditions in which the interviewers will be operating and what type of equipment is best suited to these situations? Given that interviewers may not always have access to electricity and other amenities, how well does the equipment operate on batteries? How rugged is it and how well does it perform in a variety of situations?

Who is available to take care of the equipment? It is helpful to know about the types of maintenance the equipment needs, how it should be done, what is most likely to need repairing, and what the possible repair costs can be. Librarians and school audio-visual staff can be helpful sources of information on equipment maintenance and repair track records.

What factors can cause loss of recorded signal and how often does this occur? One of the greatest fears of oral historians is to find out, too late, that the great interview just completed didn't record because of equipment problems. It is always helpful to ask how to identify factors leading to possible equipment or media recording malfunctions. You will also want to ask, should the worst happen, how much information lost due to malfunctioning equipment or media you can expect to retrieve with the equipment you want to use, how this is done, what the cost of doing it is, and who is available to do it.

Including video in an oral history project is an important decision. Here are some questions to help you make that decision.

What is your project budget and how will video enhance the final result? Videotaping can be more expensive than audiotaping. As with audiotaping, however, the use of broadcast-quality equipment—the camera, the external microphones, and media—is the industry standard. How can you best maximize project resources? If limited resources exist, where and how will video fit best? What is most useful for your project and why? Does every interview need to be videotaped? Why or why not? Could it benefit the project to combine audio and video recordings, using video to complement or supplement the audio where it is most useful? How will the audio back-up be made and who will do it?

Who and what will be filmed? Will video provide only talking heads or will it be used to provide a visual element that complements or provides additional background to the information being collected? If video provides talking heads, how will this further the goals of your project? How will your project benefit from the use of video and how is this reconciled with overall needs and budget resources?

Are camera operators or videographers available if needed to make video recordings and how accessible are they to your project? What is their experience with oral history? What is the cost of using them?

Who will conduct the video interviews and what experience does this person have with video oral history? Just as audio interviews should be researched and organized, video interviews must be carefully planned. The purpose of video interviews is to collect audio and visual information that enhances knowledge about the interview topics. Video interviews are usually done by the interviewer working alone or with one person on a camera. The interviewer is in charge of the interview and makes final decisions on such factors as set, lighting, and camera angles.

What are the possible needs at the recording site, such as special lenses, lighting, microphones, cables and accessories, and necessary power sources? If these are not readily available, it will be helpful for you to find out how to provide for each.

How will a video recording session affect the narrator and interviewer? It is helpful to think about the presence of video equipment and whether it will distract the narrator, preventing successful interaction between interviewer and narrator during the interview. It is also helpful to be aware of possible effects of video recording equipment on the interviewer and to try to incorporate video interviewing techniques into interviewer training sessions whenever video will be used.

What are the recording conditions for use of video? If the interview is to be recorded outdoors, do you know how this will affect the final interview product? How does this contrast with the use of a studio, the narrator's home or place of business, or other indoor settings? It is helpful to find out how to maintain broadcast quality audio and video standards in each setting. What will result in video that furthers project goals?

What are the wishes of the narrators? Do the narrators understand they will be videotaped? Do they understand how the project plans to use the video? Do they understand there can be additional uses of the video in the future?

Will video be useful for future projects and is this a determining factor for your project? You may want to think about the possible future uses of video interviews and then decide if meeting undefined future needs is part of your project goal or purpose.

WHAT SHOULD YOU KNOW ABOUT RECORDING TECHNOLOGY AND ONGOING ACCESS TO INTERVIEW MATERIALS?

Access questions are major factors to consider when developing a project and choosing equipment. This becomes especially obvious as soon as you want to use interview materials for a specific project, such as a museum exhibit or Internet site.

Although the fundamental purpose of oral history is the development of primary source materials documenting firsthand information, project coordinators increasingly consider audio or video products as an important project outcome. Oral history materials are also being sought more often for audio or video uses beyond those designed into the

project. The use of broadcast-quality equipment is critical in all these cases.

Key access questions relate to potential uses of the materials, the choice of repository, and interview processing techniques. Oral history projects typically record interviews for both immediate and long-term use, although immediate use, such as a publication, audiovisual program, or museum exhibit, more often drives project development. With this in mind, the type of project and the need to quickly and easily gain access to oral history materials become factors in choosing equipment.

Several issues involved in choosing a repository were discussed previously. This choice can also have an impact on access through the types of storage facilities available, policies relating to care of materials, and internal decisions that affect availability.

You will also want to think about processing techniques, whether done through the project or by repository staff. These techniques are discussed in detail in chapter 10, but in brief, they follow one of two forms: full transcription or development of an abstract and tape log. Full transcription is writing down what was said during the interview word-for-word. It provides the most complete and ongoing access to interview information and often includes a subject index. A tape log is a list of each subject discussed during the interview noting the specific time it was said (usually determined by a stopwatch). Digital media devices often come with a time code recorded on a separate track.

The following project planning questions involving access refer to audio and video, whether analog or digital:

For digital equipment, is the software and hardware you are using proprietary (unavailable for use without permission from the owner) or is it open and standard?

What about format obsolescence? In other words, what happens when the software and hardware systems you are using are no longer available? How will this affect access?

Is the media backwards compatible and, if so, for how many generations?

Is a CODEC needed to read digitally recorded information and what do you know about its providing ongoing access to the materials?

What features do the equipment and media offer and how will these benefit both the project and future uses of the materials? For example, digital information can be easily edited with a computer. Is it necessary to record the interviews in digital format, or should materials be recorded on analog tapes and transferred to digital for specific programming uses?

Who will be responsible for the oral history collection at the repository? What experience do they have handling oral history materials and in handling your formats?

What equipment does the repository keep on hand to play the tapes or discs when needed? What software and hardware systems does the digital equipment use? What are the repository's policies for maintaining equipment and software and hardware systems to play digitally recorded tapes or discs?

What are the plans for making copies of the interviews and for keeping the originals as the preservation masters, which is important regardless of the type of media you use? What equipment is available for copying? What medium will interviews be copied into and why? What are the resources for making user copies of the material?

Who will be processing the information in the interview and what equipment is available for this purpose? What type of processing (developing a transcript or a tape log) will be done and what types of processing equipment are needed? What medium should materials be in for processing? What will it take to put the recorded interview material into a format for processing? If full transcripts are to be made (important for both audio and video interviews), access to the contents of the interview will probably be ongoing. But if you decide to rely on a tape log, how will continued access be maintained to the spoken information to which the tape log is keyed?

Do the digital recorders you are considering conform to national and international standards regarding basic specifications, interchangeability, and compatibility among brands? How do you plan to use information in the interviews? While collecting oral history will add primary source material to repositories, oral history interviews are often used to provide material for museum exhibits, radio and television programs, World Wide Web sites, and written materials, among many other uses. What are some possible uses of the interviews beyond primary source documents? What formats would make them more useful and what kinds of personnel, equipment, and budget would be needed to put the interviews into these formats?

Do you have plans to put project materials on the Internet or on digital TV? You may be interested in streaming (playing sound or video over the Internet). Material on the Internet can also easily be moved to digital TV. Keeping in mind the Internet does not replace the need for a permanent repository for project materials, what formats are needed for Web site development? What are your reasons for putting project information on the World Wide Web and how do they further overall project development? What are the steps and costs needed to put project materials into a format for use on the World Wide Web? How do Web-related needs affect other access issues?

WHAT SHOULD YOU KNOW ABOUT RECORDING TECHNOLOGY AND LONGEVITY OF THE INTERVIEWS?

Although it is sometimes difficult to think about the needs of researchers and others well into the future, the purpose of oral history is to collect and preserve information that could otherwise be lost. Once collected, this primary source material is as important and unique as an old diary or as letters dating back hundreds of years. Just as people today still read first-person accounts about life on the Oregon Trail through diaries and letters written by nineteenth-century travelers, people in the future will turn to oral histories to learn from the information they contain. Adherence to good archival standards will ensure the oral history information you record is as accessible in the future as the centuries-old diaries are today.

Planning for longevity of the interview and the information it contains is one of the most important parts of the oral history process. It can also be one of the most difficult and confusing. Bruce Bruemmer, archivist at Cargill, Inc., pointed out in a 1991 *American Archivist* article that "oral historians are [often] producers, not curators."[11] This dilemma is reflected in what may be referred to as the contradictory needs of historic records maintenance. Paul Eisloeffel, media curator at the Nebraska State Historical Society, notes that archivists are responsible for the long-term care of records and media that may have been created originally for a more immediate purpose. The challenge, then, is long-term care and maintenance of materials created in a variety of formats using a variety of media, each of which has its own preservation needs. This is even more of an issue today, when oral historians have a variety of equipment types, software and hardware systems, and tapes and discs from which to choose. The challenge includes caring for and maintaining information in both spoken and written forms.

As software, hardware, and media change and are updated, archivists and others owning oral history materials will want to think about maintaining access to the information in both the original format and in the most up-to-date formats. Maintaining information in the original format, especially if analog, preserves the most accurate recording available in a format that requires little in the way of advanced technology to retrieve. Many institutions also regularly transfer materials to newer formats. The transfer processes are called digitizing (transferring analog to digital), refreshing (recreating files on new software-hardware systems), reformatting (moving files to software-hardware systems with different specifications), and migrating (moving data between media). Archivists recommend digitized items be transferred to the latest formats every five years to keep up with changes in technology.

Whether you are thinking about analog or digital, audio or video, consider these long-term access issues for oral history materials:

What are the repository's policies for long-term access to oral history materials (digital and analog, audio and video) in its collections? Is the software and hardware used to record the materials still on the market? If not, how will the repository handle access? Realizing analog is less complex than digital, what are the policies for long-term access to each? A compact disc may last a century or more, but the software and hardware to play it may be obsolete tomorrow.

What are staff and budget priorities for care of analog and digital materials, including ongoing access to refreshment technology, commitment to refreshing collections, and number of copies made?

What are the staff and budget priorities for storage, and what kinds of storage facilities are available for the collections to maximize shelf life?

If the repository has collections in several digital formats, what are its policies for maintaining access to each? Does it have collections in the various formats? What are staff and budget priorities for this? What are its policies and priorities for standardizing formats and what does this involve in budget and staff time?

What are the most recent archival staff recommendations regarding long-term stability of your chosen format (digital and analog)? What are the most recent archival staff recommendations for long-term access to oral history tapes (analog and digital) and discs? This information may be obtained through local historical organizations if available, the media archivist at your state historical society, or the Oral History Association.

Deciding what equipment to use can be a thorny issue for oral historians. While the above discussion should help you make an informed decision about your interview needs as well as accessibility and longevity issues for the information you collect, keep in mind that this discussion highlights ideal—and hence, expensive—choices. The first priority for many projects is acquiring a broadcast-quality microphone and cable. If immediate acquisition of a full assortment of broadcast-quality equipment is not an option, at least start with these basics. If your budget is tight, you might find that equipment can be donated or loaned to a project. Schools, two- and four-year colleges, and universities often have media centers with good recording equipment and might also be sources of help or support.

Whether purchasing equipment or working with loaned equipment, the above discussion and lists of questions will help you make the best choices for your project within your budget. Do everything you reasonably can to record the interviews with the best equipment possible. And, always remember that although recording technology changes rapidly, informed and thoughtful equipment decisions during the oral history planning process will enhance the immediate and long-term uses of an oral history project.

Notes

1. Information on the history of recording was taken from the following sources: *Off the Record: The Technology and Culture of Sound Recording in America*, by David Morton (New Brunswick, N.J.: Rutgers University Press, 2000) and from several Internet sites: "Audio-Visual Preservation Resources," "Time-Line of Common Sound Recording Formats," and "Recording Technology History," by Steven E. Schoenherr, notes revised August 2, 2001. Schoenherr is the author of *Multimedia and History*, 3d ed. (Newark: University of Delaware, 1976).

2. Definitions for technical terms in this chapter are drawn from *The Dictionary of Computing and Digital*

Media: Terms & Acronyms: 1999 Edition, by Brad Hansen (Wilsonville: ABF Content, 1999).

3. Donald A. Ritchie, "Remembering Forrest Pogue," in the *Oral History Association Newsletter* 31(1) (Winter 1997): 7.

4. Brad Hansen, *The Dictionary of Multimedia Terms & Acronyms* (Wilsonville: Franklin, Beedle & Associates, 1997), 58.

5. Edward D. Ives, *The Tape-Recorded Interview*, 2d ed. (Knoxville: University of Tennessee Press, 1995).

6. Hansen, *The Dictionary of Computing and Digital Media*, 82.

7. Disc is sometimes spelled disk. We have chosen the first spelling as the more common.

8. Hansen, *The Dictionary of Computing and Digital Media*, 83.

9. James E. Fogerty, "Balancing the Content and the Container: Defining the Role of Artifacts in the Digital Age," in *Library Collections, Acquisitions, and Technical Services* 24 (2000): 251–65.

10. Donald A. Ritchie, *Doing Oral History* (New York: Twayne Publishers, 1995), 109.

11. Bruce A. Bruemmer, "Access to Oral History: A National Agenda," in *American Archivist* 54 (1991): 494–501.

CHAPTER 6

Creating a Budget and Finding Financial Support

Where can you find financial support for your oral history project? Oral historians ask that question almost as often as they ask what equipment to use. Oral history is not cheap. Committed volunteers can help underwrite the costs of a project and provide considerable manpower. But unless everything—time and materials—is donated, projects need cash to survive.

Oral history is labor-intensive work. If you think only in terms of interview costs, the project will be woefully underfunded. Although its most visible product, the interview, may only take several hours, careful preparation beforehand and meticulous processing afterward are time-consuming. Adequate budgeting for that time plus the cost of equipment and other supplies are key to successfully completing an oral history project. Identifying complete project costs and sources of revenue can make the difference between a good idea and a successfully completed project.

The full costs of an oral history project are not immediately obvious, as many project organizers have found to their dismay. The following elements should be included in an oral history project's budget:

Equipment (a one-time expense that will depend on the number of each item you need):

- recorders, including carrying cases
- microphones and accessories, including cables
- cassettes or discs for each interview and for all copies that will need to be made
- equipment for duplicating tapes or discs
- transcribing equipment (if your project plans to complete verbatim transcripts)

Overhead costs:

- administration, including the time of the project coordinators, correspondence, record-keeping, and advisory board meetings when necessary

- interviewer training
- photocopying
- postage
- telephone, fax
- printing letterhead, business cards, or project brochures
- office space
- office equipment, such as file cabinets

Interview process:

- research and preparation time
- time to arrange the interviews
- interviews
- payment to interviewers (unless interviewers are volunteers)
- payment to videographer, if used
- interview processing (both audio and video)
- time to audit-check the transcribing
- travel (interview research and/or interview)
- transcribers or tape indexers

Equipment is a one-time project expense. Once purchased, it will be available for the duration of the project. The number of recorders and microphones you will need will be based on the size of the project and the number of interviewers you will use. The number of cassettes or discs will depend on the number of narrators you'll be interviewing. Plan to make at least three copies of each preservation master: a processing copy, a public user copy, and a courtesy copy for the narrator. Procedures for purchasing equipment will be affected by your sponsoring organization's purchasing rules, particularly if you are working for a division of state or local government, such as a public library or museum, or an academic institution. Photocopying, printing, and postage are standard project costs and will depend on the size and scope of the project. Travel costs should cover both research and interview needs.

Processing costs support making copies of the interview masters as well as abstracting and indexing or transcribing. Of the two options for processing oral history interviews, transcribing is the ideal—but most expensive—option. A transcript is a verbatim written copy of everything said in the interview, audit-checked (a comparison of the written and spoken materials) for accuracy both in translating the spoken word to the written and for the correct spelling of all proper names and other specific details mentioned in the interview. It provides the most complete and long-lasting access to interview information.

If you cannot transcribe the interviews, your budget at least should include plans for an abstract and a tape log. This is a two-step process and is usually done by the interviewer or someone designated to take on this task. The first step is to listen carefully to the full interview and then write a detailed one- or two-page abstract or summary of information in the interview, paying careful attention to correct spelling of all proper names. The second step is to develop a tape log. If you plan to pay for processing the interviews, development of an abstract and tape log is generally reimbursed per hour, while transcribers are often paid either by the page or by the interview hour (a set fee for each hour of original interview transcribed, regardless of how long it takes).

Personnel costs vary, depending on project participants. Is this a volunteer-run project, a project run by paid staff, or a combination of the two? Project staff usually are paid by the hour except for interviewers, who are often paid by the interview. Transcribers are usually paid by the interview hour or transcript page. Videographers often are paid by the hour, studio hour, or interview. Narrators are not paid, although in some circumstances a gift may be given.

Oral history projects often rely on volunteers. It is an interesting process that attracts many people. However, to do it well requires firm resolve and many hours of time on the part of all project participants. In a volunteer-dependent project, everyone involved should agree to designate one or two people who are able to make a commitment for its entire duration as coordinators or planners. All volunteers then should make every effort to keep to the schedules and guidelines they establish. Projects in which this understanding has been well defined from the beginning have the best chance of success.

Oral history training is an essential expense, especially when using volunteers. A workshop for project participants, including planners, interviewers, and processors, can save everyone unnecessary mistakes and loss of time. Attending a one-day workshop to learn and practice appropriate interviewing techniques should be a minimum expectation for volunteers who want to be involved in a project, and your budget should reflect those costs.

When determining project size and feasibility, start by identifying all the costs associated with an interview. For this purpose, assume each interview will be no more than two hours long (a maximum length for oral history interviews). Per-interview costs can include:

- prorated coordinator's costs,
- prorated equipment cost,
- cassettes or discs needed to record one interview and to make copies for processing, for public use, and for the narrator,
- prorated training,
- research and preparation payment for all involved personnel,
- interviewer payment,
- support staff payments,
- prorated photocopying of research materials,
- postage to send letters to the narrator confirming the time and place of the interview and, after the interview, thanking him or her and sending a review copy of the transcript,
- travel and per diem costs,
- videographer, and
- processing.

Realizing that actual costs vary greatly by region, a figure based on the above list will give you a realistic rule-of-thumb for what a typical interview will cost. Multiplying per-interview costs by the number of interviews the project will include should give planners a ballpark project cost estimate. If salaried staff are used, personnel costs should be substituted for costs of individual positions. It can take up to thirty hours (or more) to plan for, develop, carry out, and process a single oral history interview.

You will want to begin to identify possible funding sources as soon as you have some idea of your expected costs. Some of the most common sources are self-funding by institutions, grants from state or local historical societies[1] or state humanities councils, and programs run through public libraries. Experienced oral historians know that while all are good options, the available amount of per-project funds from each of these sources is often relatively small.

Competition is keen for grants from national sources. The National Endowment for the Humanities, for example, funds oral history projects, although such projects have to show evidence of national significance, must pass rigorous reviews, and must show strong evidence of planning and preparation. Many projects look for funds from other sources to support initial planning work before considering an application for federal funds. For more information about NEH, check the Web site www.neh.gov.

In addition to the well-known and ongoing oral history programs at several colleges and universities, other academic institutions support occasional oral history projects through various departments. And teachers in elementary and secondary schools sometimes can identify special funding sources to integrate oral history projects into the curriculum. Professional associations, businesses, and interest groups related to a project's theme also are potential sources of financial support. Local governments and corporations based in your area may be other sources.

City and state-based foundations can be sources for funds, although most don't routinely fund oral history. The better planned a project is and the more carefully defined its outcomes, the more competitive it can be. Check for information about state and local funding sources at your library. Some coordinators find private sources, but if you do, take care to insure that the donors do not influence project results.

Chapter 5 provides detailed information about the types of equipment and recording cassettes or discs recommended for oral history projects. The standards are high because using good equipment maximizes the life of the interview. But don't be deterred by the price tag and think that you must abandon the project if you cannot immediately go out and purchase such equipment. Often, you can find sources of support in the community to help. Organizations that may not be able or willing to fund interviews might fund equipment purchases.

Funding and Support Suggestions

An oral history project can be an expensive undertaking. If available, volunteers can help offset some expenses. Other sources of funding and support can include:

Civic organizations: A group may want to sponsor the project, providing printing, postage, photocopying, tapes, discs—or funds.

Local businesses: Sometimes local businesses are willing to support a community effort through gifts of photocopying, postage, fax, and other administrative needs.

Radio and television stations: Both have to document community service as part of their licensing requirements. They may be willing to help with equipment.

Schools (secondary and post-secondary): They may have equipment to loan to a project. Parent groups or service clubs may also be willing to sponsor a project.

Libraries and historical societies: Both may have resources to give to a project. They may also help identify possible grant sources and provide grant-writing expertise.

Newspapers: They may be willing to help provide publicity.

Other agencies, including radio and television stations, school districts, or state historical societies might be willing to loan equipment to the project or permit you to use specialized equipment such as that needed to duplicate tapes or discs. Borrowing equipment, in fact, is sometimes preferable to buying it.

Finding funding sources does not mean just looking for outright grants, but identifying any and all possible means of support. Local businesses might provide in-kind support for equipment, cassettes or discs, printing, postage, or photocopying. Each helps defray real project costs. Community-based organizations may be willing to help with travel expenses and transcribing interviews. All can help assure successful completion of a project.

Project coordinators should keep careful record of gifts and loans of materials and time because in-kind support can help show potential funders the value of commitment to the project. Start keeping track of all time and materials used beginning with the first planning meetings and continue this practice throughout the life of the project.

Oral history project support need not come only in the form of dollars. Educational institutions often develop and carry out oral history projects, as do libraries, archives, and museums. Several major colleges and universities have ongoing, flagship programs with work done primarily by faculty and research assistants. On the other hand, the oral history project at Carleton College in Northfield, Minnesota, is an example of a volunteer program run by and for school alumnae with support from the college archives. Community members interested in documenting specific events or time periods may want to explore college or university programs to discuss possible collaborative efforts.

Local secondary school history or social studies teachers are another possible source of support. Although class schedules and days are full for students and teachers, the possibility of school-community collaboration may be of interest. Teachers across the country, such as Michael A. Brooks at Suva Intermediate School in Bell Gardens, California, successfully integrate oral history into the curriculum, offering students an exciting opportunity for hands-on learning while preserving community history that might otherwise be lost.

Keep in mind the purpose of the project you want to develop and, while gratefully accepting help and support, don't let the wishes of supporters influence project outcomes. This is not easy, but is important to the final results.

This discussion of budgeting for an oral history project does not include the costs of creating products from oral history interviews, such as Web sites, museum exhibits, books, pamphlets, or CDs. It focuses only on the development of the oral history interview as a primary source document. If you wish to develop additional products after the project has been completed, you will want to budget for this, too.

Support for oral history projects varies depending on the community, project coordinators, and available resources. As with all stages of project development, however, good planning will help. Always let potential supporters know what you want to accomplish and why it is important. Show them a clear plan of work and a realistic, clearly defined budget. Explain what the results of the project will be and how the oral history materials will be made available in the future. Finding funding is one of the most time-consuming parts of project coordination, but it can be one of the most rewarding.

Notes

1. The American Association for State and Local History (AASLH) and AltaMira Press publish the *Directory of Historical Organizations in the United States and Canada*. For more information, please see chapter 12.

CHAPTER 7

Interview Preparation

What is the best way for you to prepare for an oral history interview? Although the interview is the most well-known and well-recognized part of the oral history process, a good interview requires thorough, behind-the-scenes preparation. Interview preparation creates the structure on which the oral history is based. In chapter 2, we provided an overview of the oral history planning process, including an outline of the interview preparation steps, but here we will discuss these steps in detail.

Interview preparation generally requires two steps: **general project research** and **narrator-specific research**. Often, people are attracted to an oral history project because they know about its subject and want to talk with people about it. It is up to project coordinators to direct this enthusiasm to the interview preparation process so that the interviews themselves will live up to everyone's expectations.

Everyone involved in the project should participate in **general project research** regardless of how much some may already know. This serves several purposes:

- brings people together so they are all working from a common set of background materials toward a common goal;

- makes participants aware of existing information and lays the groundwork for defining good oral history questions to fill in gaps;

- familiarizes interviewers with enough information about the subject to be able to keep the interview on track and spot the need for follow-up questions; and

- prepares interviewers on details, such as names and dates, which can facilitate a good interview.

BEGIN BACKGROUND RESEARCH

The watchword on oral history projects is **research**. Research is essential for taking the project from the level of merely recording reminiscences to collecting the depth of information needed for good oral history. It is an important step even for those who are experts. Research helps define the project, pro-

vides background on topics to help focus them further, helps project leaders determine which topics are most important, suggests additional topics, and provides background information to inform the interviewer so he or she will be as prepared as possible for the interview.

Planners can help with this stage of project development by pulling together a basic information packet for all participants. This can include copies of written histories, newspaper articles, maps, photographs, excerpts from letters, diaries, and other primary source materials, and drawings. It can include as much information about the defined subject of the oral history project as planners deem necessary but should not be overwhelming.

With the packet of information as a base, project participants may wish to do additional research. This can include visits to the public library, historical society, newspaper archives, and specific places that have materials relevant to the project. Depending on the topics, this may involve research in local, state, or national facilities. Project advisory board members may help by finding collections to review and in identifying possible topics. The goal of all background research is to give project participants, especially the interviewers, a good base of knowledge to use in the interviews. If an interviewer is thoroughly prepared, the end product will be stronger.

Research for a project may be done by making notes with pencil and paper, note cards, or computers. In any case, it is always important to write down or enter any information that relates to the purpose of the oral history project. This includes names (with proper spellings), dates, facts, figures, and information (correct or incorrect) already on the record.[1] Interviewers will want to add to their basic packets any new information they find. All of this can help not only in defining interview topics, but in later development of specific questions.

It is always important to indicate clearly the source of the information. Keeping unclear notes often results in having to go back to clarify things—a waste of time. Many projects photocopy information if they can afford it, which can help with note taking. Photocopies, when properly identified and cited, are often a helpful addition to a project's collections. Even if projects have photocopy budgets to support research, project participants should remember to photocopy only information that pertains specifically to the subject, rather than every item reviewed.

It is usually helpful to begin the research by looking into topics on the list. Which ones are already well documented? Is the documentation complete? Are there discrepancies among various sources of information? What is already on the record and not in need of further attention during an oral history interview? What information is missing or inaccurate and should be covered in an oral history interview? What topics are not documented well at all? How important is it to document them? What questions should be asked about a topic? What subtopics come to light that help define each topic further? What questions need to be asked about a subtopic?

Research will probably bring up new topics as well. As new topics come to light, they can be added to the list and the same questions applied to them. Review of information will help project leaders determine what should be covered in the interviews and why this information should be collected.

COMPILE A BIBLIOGRAPHY

Project participants should keep a list of all information sources they use. This will be compiled as the project bibliography. It becomes an end product of the oral history project, and serves both as a reference tool for newcomers to the project and as a source for future researchers who want to know what background information created the foundation for the interviews.

DEVELOP A LIST OF DATES AND EVENTS

Working with the background information, one person or a small group should develop a project outline, identifying milestones important to the topic. Not only will this encourage everyone to focus on the materials, it will result in a useful resource document that helps guide continuing research. When you're ready to begin the interviews, it also serves as a good interviewing tool.

MAKE A LIST OF THEMES OR TOPICS TO INCLUDE IN THE INTERVIEW

In addition to giving project participants information about the subject, general background research helps planners identify topics or areas where information is sketchy or ambiguous or reveals mysterious, unanswered questions. These are all topics you'll want to cover in the oral history interviews. Oral history is used to document information that otherwise is unavailable and subject to loss. It is inefficient to use this time to record information already on the record. By familiarizing themselves with existing information, interviewers can identify gaps in what is already available and determine how to fill them through oral history.

Background researchers should keep a list of topics either lacking or inadequately covered in the written materials and any other topic ideas to include in an interview (fig 7.1). Coordinators should regularly look over these lists, analyzing how each topic relates to the mission statement. All ideas that meet the criteria should be included on a master interview topic list. Review and analyze these lists regularly to keep the project focused. They will become the basis for designing the oral history interviews.

IDENTIFY POTENTIAL NARRATORS AND DETERMINE THEMES OR TOPICS TO COVER WITH EACH OF THEM

General project research is an essential way to identify potential narrators. Although you might know from the outset some of the people you'll want to interview, general background research often leads to others whose knowledge is essential to project success. Background research will also help identify additional, perhaps previously unknown, types of information needed to fill gaps in knowledge, leading project coordinators to seek out potential narrators with this knowledge. The background research also can help you decide which people might have enough information for several interview sessions, while others might require only a shorter, single interview session.

As a rule of thumb, don't start out by planning an overly ambitious number of interviews. If your initial goal is to interview everyone whose name surfaces, the task will be so daunting, everyone involved will be frustrated and defeated from the start. Instead, begin with no more than three to five interviews—up to ten recorded hours. Set a goal of ensuring these are well researched, well structured, and fully processed. When this is done, look at what it took to meet this goal and determine what is most manageable for your group to continue with

Sample List of Names and Dates

1901	Brothers Martin and Marvin Jones develop a product for preventing power loss in engines. The Jones brothers were awarded a patent on their invention.
1902	The Jones Production Company was incorporated with an issue of 100,000 shares of capital stock at $.75/share.
1909	Everett Smith joined the company as general operations manager. He developed the major market for the product.
1914	The company became known as Jones Company, Inc.
1918	The company received its first government contract.
1921	The company employed 350 people prior to the "farm crash" and the start of the agricultural depression.
1927	The company began to diversify its product line by adding smaller sizes in an attempt to stave off losses.
1934	The company was sold to Charles Anderson and Sons.
1939	The company began making engines that featured its product.
1940	The company received a government contract to make engines using its product. It employed 750 people working three shifts.
1944	The company received an award for its war work.
1945	The plant voted to unionize under the leadership of John Ross.
1949	Charles Anderson retired and his sons, John and George, took over company management.
1950	The company built a new plant at 37th and Randolph Streets. The old plant at 12th and Elm Streets was torn down and the land was sold to the city. Employment was at 450 people working two shifts.
1953	The company received a government contract to build engines.
1956	The company negotiated a deal with Montgomery Ward to distribute engines through their stores.
1959	The union staged a major strike for better wages and conditions. The strike lasted for 3 months and resulted in raises up to $3.00 per hour and increased safety procedures.
1962	The plant burned to the ground.
1964	The plant was re-built and had its grand opening. The product line was expanded to include engine-related products. Employment was at 300.
1968	The workforce was fully integrated for the first time.
1973	The Anderson brothers sold the company to a XYZ Company, Inc., a national distributor of engines and related equipment.
1979	Sales were affected by the Energy Crisis. Employment at 200.
1985	XYZ Company expanded the product line to include engine-related equipment from plants it owned in other states.
1991	XYZ Company sold the company to Engines International, Ltd., a London-based manufacturing company.
1998	Engines International, Ltd. sold its holdings, including the company, to Sheridan, Inc., an international conglomerate.
2002	The company celebrated its centennial. Employment at 375.

Figure 7.1. A sample list of dates and events for an oral history project.

additional interviews. A handful of well-done interviews can inspire confidence in the project and energize participants to keep going. Having something concrete to show for your efforts also can generate more financial support for future work.

Oral history focuses on collecting firsthand knowledge. As such, narrators should be selected because of their knowledge about the interview themes and topics. They also should represent a variety of perspectives and backgrounds about the themes or topics. In fact, it is often the purpose of an oral history project specifically to seek out perspectives that are not already on the record. This will enhance the results of your oral history project, broadening the base of information you collect.

A project Edward Nelson, Robert "Skip" Drake, and others developed several years ago in Minnesota to collect information about the Civilian Conservation Corps (CCC), for example, easily could have used all of its available resources interviewing the men who enrolled in the camps. The network was still strong, relatively little documentation was on the written record about enrollees' time in the CCC camps, and narrators could be found quickly because many were willing to tell their stories. But they could only tell one part of the story. This oral history project included others, such as: U.S. Army personnel who ran the work camps in which the enrollees lived; representatives from the agencies that developed the projects enrollees worked on, including former forest service personnel, state park officials, and others involved with various conservation projects or agencies; adult work leaders and crew leaders assigned to supervise enrollees at work; and members of racial or ethnic groups who were or were not welcomed into the camps. Making an effort to include all sides of the issues enhances the project and gives it the depth that characterizes oral history.

Lists of possible narrators are sometimes easily formed. At other times, it can take considerable legwork to find people who have firsthand knowledge about the project's themes or topics and who are good prospective narrators. In addition to relying on project research to uncover names of possible narrators, advisory board members and informal networks of individuals knowledgeable about the project and its purpose can add to the list. Depending on the subject, informal networks can generate a long list of possible narrators that will have to be winnowed down to a manageable size.

Good narrators for an oral history interview are people who:

- have firsthand, previously undocumented information about project topics or themes;
- represent all sides of an issue;
- have strong powers of observation;
- have a good memory;
- can communicate effectively;
- have an ability to understand the basics of the oral history process as explained by the interviewer or project coordinator and are willing to participate in all its phases, including signing a donor form;
- are willing to give an account of their memories of the project topics or themes; and
- are reasonably comfortable with interview equipment in either audio or video settings.

Narrators bring their own biases to project topics or themes. Their memories also reflect their perspectives on what happened, the ways in which they have organized their understanding of the past, and their frames of reference on what is or is not important. They are also often influenced by thoughts and ideas that have occurred since the event or time period. You will want to be aware of this while realizing a narrator is chosen for a project because his or her views about it are important. Each narrator brings a unique perspective to the project's topics or themes, and collectively, those perspectives enrich the historical record.

It is often helpful to think about choosing possible narrators in terms of the information each can bring to your project. Narrators may be chosen for knowledge about a certain time period or because they represent a certain perspective about an event related to the themes or topics. They may be chosen because they have a long-time perspective, although, while you will want to take age and health factors into consideration, it is never necessary to interview the oldest person around just because they're old. They may be chosen because of their knowledge about information related to the themes or topics, although it is also not always necessary to interview the most visible local historian or the most famous person associated with an event. Often, in fact, such local notables have either told or written their story many times and it is already a part of the existing record. Sometimes they have repeated the stories so often, almost as a rehearsed performance, that it's impossible for them to move into the deeper exploration of the event that marks good oral history. Project coordinators should, instead, look for people who have firsthand knowledge and are willing to communicate this information clearly and effectively, answering the interviewer's questions to the best of their ability.

The names of potential narrators should go into a pool for discussion and analysis. Depending on your project's resources, choices will have to be made. The most helpful approach is to determine priority, identifying narrators whom you think are most critical to include and working down the list as resources are available. Although you may identify additional criteria based on the needs of a project, a person's ability to provide information about the interview topics should be the primary factor when choosing narrators. Using this as a guide to match potential narrators to interview topics about which they are most knowledgeable will help organize the project and will ensure inclusion of narrators whose information is most useful.

Project participants, including the coordinators, should decide who will be interviewed. Although supporters and others interested in the project will have ideas about potential narrators, project coordinators and interviewers who have been involved in the research are in the best position to know who should be interviewed and what the interview priorities should be. Names of potential narrators will continue to surface as the project progresses, and the narrator list and priorities could change based on this new information. It is not a good idea to advertise for narrators. You should reserve the right to determine who will be on the final narrator list. A public solicitation for narrators often carries with it the implied promise of an interview, which may hamper the project's final results.

Once possible narrators have been identified, project coordinators should begin contacting them, requesting their involvement in the project. This is usually done with a letter explaining the project and providing background about their expected involvement. A sample letter, along with samples of all suggested correspondence, is included in appendix 3. The designated interviewer should follow up the letter with a telephone call. This provides an opportunity for the interviewer and narrator to talk informally, allows the interviewer to answer addi-

tional questions, and gives the narrator a chance to make a verbal commitment to be interviewed. Some narrators, when first contacted, may be unsure of their ability to contribute effectively to the project. The telephone call can also allow the interviewer to address these questions and concerns.

After the first narrators have agreed to be a part of the project, interviewers should begin **narrator-specific research**. This step creates the structure for the interview. An interviewer should work on only one interview at a time, selecting or being assigned narrators in priority order from the pool of names.

Narrator-specific research involves learning as much as possible about the person to be interviewed and his or her role in the subject at hand. This may include such details as work history, personal history, family history, political history—anything that gives the interviewer the necessary background to ask good project-related questions with appropriate follow-up. Such research also helps build rapport between interviewer and narrator during the interview. The interviewer should rely on as wide a variety of background materials as necessary to become fully informed. This often includes review of related interviews and trips to the historical society, library, newspaper office, and other sites containing resource information. It may also include review of maps, visits to sites that are important to the interview, and additional work with primary sources.

It may be difficult to find documented information about a narrator. Whether this is the case or not, narrator-specific research can focus on the context of the narrator's background to give the interviewer as much knowledge as possible. Asking the narrator to provide biographical information prior to the interview also can help by making available additional information to guide the research.

DEVELOP AN INTERVIEW OUTLINE

Using the master topic list as a guide and combining it with information obtained in your narrator-specific research, the interviewer develops the **interview outline**. This is not a scripted list of questions. It is a list of topics to cover in the interview, often combined with notes the interviewer will find helpful in eliciting information in the most professional way possible. Project coordinators should review the interviewer's guide to make sure topics covered are consistent with the project's goals.

After defining the interview focus, the interviewer should think about narrator-specific topics that can help structure the interview. These can be organized on the interview outline by sequence of events. It is helpful to list the topics in the order the narrator may want to discuss them. Many interviewers find that approaching topics chronologically is helpful, since that is how people often think. If the questions are likely to include emotionally charged or sensitive topics, it's usually best to plan for those later in the interview, after you've had a chance to establish rapport with the narrator. Regardless of the order of the topics listed on the outline, the interviewer should follow the narrator's train of thought and remain flexible in how and when topics are introduced.

Within each subject area, the interviewer should list the points to be covered and background information about each. This will help identify the specifics to be discussed during the interview while providing the interviewer with details about existing information. The outline should be organized so the interview will flow smoothly from one topic to another while allowing for the inclusion of information that may be unexpected and yet relevant to the project.

The interview outline should reflect the purpose of the project. For example, if the focus of an interview were on a person's experiences as a nurse in the Korean War, the interviewer probably would not take interview time to ask detailed, in-depth questions about union involvement or farming activities, though the person may have much information on those subjects, too. Similarly, any pre-interview contacts or correspondence with the narrator would make clear that the Korean War nursing experiences would be the focus of the interview. Based on what is already known about the designated subject of an oral history project, the interviewer will want to concentrate on eliciting information the narrator can add that fits overall project goals.

The interview outline should contain as much information as the interviewer needs for the interview. This can include notes about names and places and dates from the research that will help stimulate the narrator's memory. It should not be so voluminous, however, that the interviewer spends more time shuffling notes and looking for details than asking questions and listening to the answers.

As seen in the sample in appendix 5, the interview outline should not be written in question for-mat and doesn't need to be in complete sentences. An oral history interview is not a scripted telemarketing survey. Listing discussion topics rather than questions encourages an easy flow of information between interviewer and narrator and helps keep the interviewer's focus on the narrator and his or her responses rather than on reading one question after another. The interviewer will want to use the information in the interview outline to frame questions, to offer specifics that help the narrator place a question in context, and to develop follow-up questions.

Interviewers should be familiar with everything in the interview guide and should know the reasons for including each topic and how each fits into overall project structure. They should be prepared to hear new, firsthand information and to clarify anything they don't immediately understand. They should also be prepared to be flexible, since a narrator might want to talk about things in a different order than listed on the interview outline. The interviewer should use the outline to ensure all topics have been fully covered. Finally, interviewers should never include opinions about what they think, either on the interview outline or during the interview. Interviewers should approach the interview as impartial, nonjudgmental facilitators who are prepared to pin down information, ask pointed questions, and probe beneath the surface for new information about the interview topics.

SCHEDULE THE INTERVIEW

When nearing completion of the narrator-specific research and development of the interview outline, the interviewer should contact the narrator to set up the interview. This may be done by telephone, but should be followed up with a letter confirming date, time, and location. The letter should also include a request for a photograph of the narrator for the master file.

Oral history projects usually include a face-to-face pre-interview or a preliminary telephone contact with potential narrators at this point. This involves a short, general discussion with the person about the interview. This step can help interviewers and narrators meet informally before the interview and gives the interviewer a chance to tell the narrator a little about himself or herself if necessary. Some interviewers like to collect biographical information from the narrator at this point. It also provides an opportunity to answer any further questions about the oral history project and to explain the recording process and the use of the donor form. And it can be a good time to discuss the interview topics in general terms with the narrator, though there are several words of caution here. Be careful not to give the narrator lists of the questions to be asked; while you may think this will help the narrator prepare for the interview, in reality it often results only in rehearsed answers, not the vibrant responses with the depth that oral history can elicit. Occasionally, narrators who have seen a complete list of questions will write out their answers, which they then will want to read into the microphone. This is not oral history. Sharing the interview outline also can inhibit inclusion of any additional information not on the outline that may add depth to the interview. And do not allow the pre-interview discussion to include the telling of specific information you want to cover in the interview. When this happens and you then ask for the information in the interview, the narrator often either refers to the earlier conversation rather than answering the question or repeats the story in a less lively way than you heard it initially. As a follow-up, the interview confirmation letter can summarize your discussion, listing the general topics to be covered in the interview.

Interviewers should be thoroughly trained on using the equipment before going on an interview. They should know how to use it unobtrusively and with confidence and how to handle minor difficulties in the field. Always begin by reading the manual that comes with the equipment. It will help you understand what all the dials, switches, and buttons mean and how each works. Specifically, pay attention to how to operate the record, stop, play, rewind, fast forward, and eject functions that control recording. You will also want to know what controls sound, what monitors sound, how to set sound levels, and how to troubleshoot (what are the proper settings for your recorder and are they all set as they should be?). Practice with the equipment

repeatedly before using it for the first time in the interview setting.

It is always helpful to have a checklist of all items needed for the interview. Such a list can include:

- recorder,
- microphone, cables, and microphone stand,
- AC adapter/transformer and extension cord,
- tapes or discs (it is wise to take more than you could possibly need),
- batteries,
- notebook (often in 6x9 steno format),
- pencil,
- folder containing the donor form (two copies—one for the master file and one to leave with the narrator), the interview outline, the biographical information form, and copies of the letters to the narrator, and
- camera to take a black-and-white picture of the narrator in interview setting (this is necessary for audio interviews and is helpful to add to the master file for video interviews).

Finally, arrive on time. A prompt arrival will start the process out right. If there has not been a pre-interview meeting, this may be the first time the interviewer and narrator meet, in which case it is even more important not to be late.

Preparation for the interview is not glamorous. Nor is it as exciting as the actual interview. Without adequate preparation, however, the oral history interview will not fulfill its potential.

Notes

1. David Kyvig and Myron Marty include several chapters of helpful, common-sense research guidelines in their book *Nearby History: Exploring the Past Around You*, 2d ed. (Walnut Creek, Calif.: AltaMira Press, 2000).

The Interview Setting

How should you arrange the interview setting? Interviews can take place in a variety of locations, ranging from central sites to the narrator's home, to schools, museums, or more formal studio locations. Many interviews take place in the narrator's home. Here the narrator is in a familiar setting, which can have a positive effect on the interview. It can be the easiest for the narrator and may make scheduling the interview a relatively smooth process.

Interviews also can take place in work settings or in other places outside the home. Before scheduling the interview in such a location, you will want to review the suggested setting. It should be a place with control over sound (and visual) quality where the narrator and interviewer can have an uninterrupted discussion. Business office locations, for example, are appropriate only if the narrator can prevent telephone interruptions. Some interviews take place in studios. These settings, which usually involve at least one more person in addition to the interviewer, may result in a more formal product. If the interview is done in a television studio, the presence of lights, cameras, and camera operator can be intimidating. In all cases, think about the purposes of the interviews and the settings that will produce results that most effectively meet your project's goals. In all cases, the interview should take place in a setting where the narrator is comfortable so that the setting itself does not create distractions or make the narrator ill at ease.

Several elements of the interview setting are standard, regardless of where the interview takes place. Although video settings have some unique needs, discussed below, the following elements apply to both audio and video.

When possible, the narrator chooses where he or she wants to be interviewed. This should be a comfortable spot, where he or she can relax and focus on the interview. The narrator should, if possible, sit in a comfortable chair that does not squeak or make other noises and is situated with few distractions around it. The interviewer will want to sit no more than six feet away, facing the narrator. The narrator should be able to hear the interviewer's voice clearly, and the interviewer should be able to maintain eye contact with the narrator. It can help to have a table next to the interviewer to hold the recorder (fig. 8.1).

The microphone should be no more than two to three feet from, and pointed at, the narrator. An omnidirectional microphone will pick up the voices of interviewer and narrator, but focusing it on the narrator will maximize the sound quality of his or her voice. Carry a long enough microphone cable to allow the best placement of both pieces of equipment.

If lavaliere microphones are used, one should be clipped on the interviewer and one on the narrator, each about ten inches from his or her mouth. These have the advantage of clearly picking up voices in the interview, but can also pick up unwanted sound from rustling clothes or clanking jewelry as a person moves.

While some related research fields focus primarily on the narrator with less emphasis on hearing the interviewer's questions, the structure of the oral history interview is critical to understanding the information in it. It is important to record both interviewer and narrator, being able to hear clearly what questions were asked and in what order. This helps future users understand the context of the interview and, thus, the information in it.

In most circumstances, the interviewer should plug the audio recorder into a wall or floor outlet. A long, heavy-duty extension cord is important for this purpose. Place it in a way to prevent anyone tripping over it. Some interviewers also carry backup batteries for the recorder to use in an emergency.

Always check for factors that affect sound quality, whether in a home or institutional setting. These can include echoes from hard surfaces on walls, floors, or furniture, sounds coming through open windows or doors, air conditioner fans, telephones ringing, appliances humming, clocks chiming, pets barking, mewing, or chirping, distracting sounds from adjacent rooms, and the many other noises people usually tune out but which the recording equipment faithfully picks up. Some places are generally quiet but have noisy times when they should not be used for interviews. As a guest, especially when the interview is recorded in someone's home,

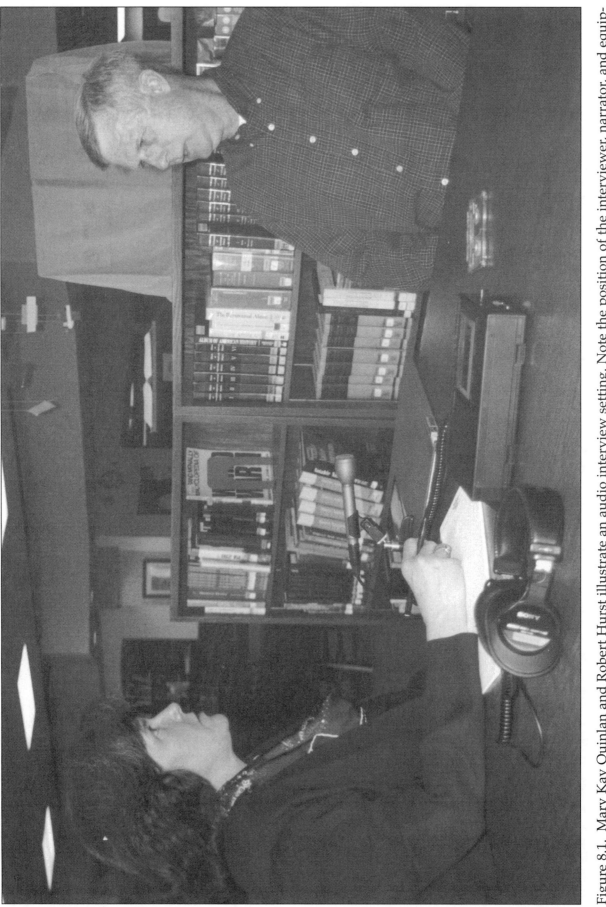

Figure 8.1. Mary Kay Quinlan and Robert Hurst illustrate an audio interview setting. Note the position of the interviewer, narrator, and equipment. *Photo credit: Ann Quinlan.*

the interviewer may be offered food or drink. Remember that the sounds of coffee cups on saucers, ice in glasses, pop tops being opened on cans, and other food consumption that occurs during the interview will be recorded and will mar the sound quality of the final product.

In many cases, interviewers can explain the situation to the narrator and elicit his or her help in maximizing sound quality. Excessive fussing, however, can get the interview off to a difficult start, while a little advance planning can help things go smoothly. The more familiar you are with the interview setting, the easier it will be to check for and control sound quality factors. This may include knowing how to turn off the telephone ringer with the narrator's permission (making sure to turn it back on after the interview), suggesting the chimes on a clock be stopped for the duration of the interview, asking the narrator not to pound a pipe on the table, or making sure there are no hard-surfaced tables that could cause sound echoes between interviewer and narrator. Relatively simple actions can often make a great deal of difference in the sound quality of the final product.

The Interview Setting

Remember to keep the interview setting as comfortable as possible. This will help the narrator concentrate on the interview.

It is important to establish rapport with the narrator. A sense of trust between narrator and interviewer helps make a good interview.

Look carefully for noise sources, such as ringing phones and chiming clocks, that will undermine the sound quality of the interview.

Take a little time with the narrator before beginning the interview to talk and relax.

Always be on time for an interview.

Always do a sound check with the equipment in the interview setting. It does not need to be long, just enough to indicate the equipment is working properly and the voices are being picked up clearly.

This is also the time for you to set sound levels on the equipment to most accurately record the narrator's voice, avoiding distortion from settings that are too high or the possible loss of sound if the settings are too low.

Waiting for an interview to begin can be a stressful time for the narrator. Hearing one's voice on tape can be unsettling in general, and hearing his or her voice on tape as part of a sound check while waiting to be asked at least an hour's worth of questions can be intimidating. You will want to be aware of this, for it can affect the narrator's responses as you start asking interview questions. Usually, asking the narrator to give his or her name and address and chatting about something neutral while unobtrusively checking recording levels will be enough without adding too much to the strain of starting the interview.

Oral historians often use headphones to continuously monitor the sound. This allows you to identify sound problems and correct them before leaving the interview. You can also use the headphones to monitor the sound check at the beginning of the interview, allowing you to make sure all is working well without having the narrator listen to the sound of his or her voice on tape just before the interview begins.

Place the recording equipment so you will have easy access to it throughout the interview. You will want to monitor it to make sure it is operating correctly and to reach it to change tapes or discs as necessary. It is best placed outside the narrator's direct line of vision to encourage his or her focus on the interviewer, but should never be hidden from view since this would raise red flags about the ethics of the interviewer and the oral history project. Oral historians do not engage in clandestine recording.

A video interview is more complicated to set up. While video can be a valuable tool to oral historians, think carefully about the best use of video in your project. Is it to record information from a well-known person whose voice *and* face are important to the project? Is it to record information from people at a specific site for a specific purpose important to the project? Is it to record information from a group of people? Is it to record one person in a studio setting, the so-called "talking head," and, if so, how will this benefit the project? Answers to these questions will help you maximize project resources regarding the use of video.

The first major consideration when deciding to use video is recording to broadcast-quality standards. This means using equipment that interviewers accustomed only to audio interviews may find unfamiliar. All but the most experienced interviewers likely would find it difficult and distracting to ask questions while operating video-recording equipment. Unless the interviewer is thoroughly trained and proficient in using the video equipment, it is usually advisable to use a videographer or camera operator to record the interview, leaving the interviewer free to conduct it.

Due to the more complex nature of the video interview, it is advisable to carefully think through decisions about the final product. What is the purpose of the interview and how does it fit into the overall oral history project? Project coordinators and the interviewer will want to determine where the interview will take place, keeping in mind the ways the setting can help meet overall project goals. Indoor or studio interviews can result in "talking heads." On-site interviews often help illustrate places important to the project.

Consider developing a more detailed interview outline when using video. This does not mean scripting what the narrator will say, but does mean carefully planning all details. How long will the interview last? What is its purpose? What information will be covered? Given possible time limitations, what information is most critical to cover? Where will the interview take place? Is there information that should be covered in a studio or at a specific site? If so, why, and how will this be handled?

Video interviews tend to be more formal than audio and can have strict time restrictions, depending on the recording circumstances. Paying for the use of a studio and hiring a videographer or camera operator, for example, might limit the interview to a specific block of time, with no flexibility to extend the session, even if the narrator still has important things to say. Because of this, it is important to make sure the interview covers the necessary material in the allotted time to the highest standard possible.

If the interview takes place indoors, be sure to provide an appropriate setting for the narrator. Shoot it in soft light that illuminates the set appropriately. Overhead lighting generally results in a poor quality video. The narrator should not sit in front of a window or other sources of natural light.

The background should not overwhelm the setting or the person being interviewed. A plain, neutral or blue backdrop often works well. Discreet props are sometimes used, but are not necessary.

Always frame the shot to be complimentary to the narrator, taking care to focus properly and to center the narrator in the picture. Give him or her what videographers call "head room" and "look space," meaning the interview is not shot at too close range. Carefully check and monitor camera angles. Most interviews are shot at eye level (matching the camera lens to the eye level of the narrator), a psychologically and emotionally neutral position. The camera should not cut the person at the neck, waist or knees. A head shot from the mid-chest or shoulders up is a common position. If the video interview is to be with more than one narrator, position groups of people so the faces of all narrators may be clearly seen and the interviewer may maintain eye contact with each person.[1]

In a video interview, ask the narrator to wear uncluttered clothing in neutral or dark colors. White shirts and blouses reflect the light and make filming natural skin tones difficult. Make sure shading works *with* the narrator, not against him or her.

As with audio interviews, information about the interview should be clearly stated at the beginning of the interview and again at the beginning of each new tape or disc. State the identifying information while simultaneously filming it before starting the interview. A visual tape slate should show, at a minimum, interviewer name, narrator name, project name, location of taping, tape number, and date. If nothing else is available, tape slate information should be handwritten on a piece of paper and filmed. If you are going to film photographs or artifacts as part of the video process, they should be shot propped up on a stand against a black background.

Inside interviews are usually shot with one camera on a tripod for stability. The focus is on the narrator and there is little or no change in the camera beyond the essentials to capture movement once the shot has been framed. Although questions should be heard clearly on the video, interviewers are generally not seen. Regardless of whether the interviewer is on camera, he or she should sit or stand, depending on the interview location, looking at the narrator with the camera over one shoulder. The narrator should talk directly to the interviewer. This camera placement allows him or her to talk to the camera as well. If project coordinators want the interviewer to be seen during the interview, more than one camera will be needed, since one camera should always be on the narrator. Check with a videographer or camera operator to determine what is needed and what the cost will be to add this option.

Lavaliere microphones are most often used for video interviews in a studio because they provide the most even sound quality. If only one lavaliere microphone is available, it should be used by the narrator, and a boom microphone should be used to pick up the interviewer's voice.

Filming on location (outside of a studio, in a natural setting) presents other needs. What visual on-site information is critical to the interview and how will it be integrated into the process? If a variety of sites or backgrounds is needed, how will each fit into the process? If on site, where specifically will the interview take place and why? What will be in the background and how will this contribute to the overall quality of the interview? What conditions are needed for optimum sound and visual quality at the place chosen for the interview and what is the best time to achieve these conditions?

As with the indoor shooting, only one camera is necessary unless there are specific project requirements or the project director has determined the interviewer should also be on film. The camera should be on a tripod for stability. Good sound control can be achieved with an external microphone on a hand-held boom (fig. 8.2).

Scout the site carefully, choosing a site to enhance the interview information while not being too distracting or intrusive for the narrator. Keep the camera on the narrator during the interview, but make a "sweeping pan" of the entire setting either before or after the interview, taking pictures of specific items or places that illustrate interview information. Guidelines on clothing and camera angles given above apply equally to on-location interviews.

When considering an outdoor video interview, pay special attention to lighting and sound. Light can change during the interview, and it is good to plan for this possibility. It is also important to try to control background sounds, such as the noise from airplanes or highways, as much as possible. Careful lighting and sound checks by the videographer or camera operator will result in a higher quality product. Always stop the interview if intrusive sounds occur and wait for conditions to return to normal.

Video interviews, whether in a studio or on site, should be recorded simultaneously on audio equipment. Use the audio recording for transcribing and as an archival back-up of the interview.

Several considerations, in addition to the greater expense of video, may affect plans for whether or how much of your interviews you record with video equipment. Video can be more intrusive than audio if large equipment is used and if the presence of additional people, such as a camera operator, is needed. These situations may inhibit the narrator, making him or her reluctant to respond openly to questions. Some people may not mind being recorded on less-intrusive digital video cameras, but this should be explored carefully before the decision is made. On the other hand, some projects might have a significant visual element, and video recording at least portions of some interviews would markedly enhance the historical documentation.

Be sure to think about possible future uses of the video. It is easier to edit and use materials with similar backgrounds, lighting, and sound characteristics. While specific future uses of the material may not be the primary reasons for doing oral history, it is good planning to maximize the quality of the interview at the time it is produced. Remember, however, that video interviews are primary source materials, not documentaries. While excerpts of materials from both video and audio interviews often are used effectively in documentaries and other productions, the interviews themselves should be kept intact and handled as primary source materials.

Thinking through the setting is an important part of the process, for it can affect the outcome of the interview. As an example, a community recently began a project documenting the placement of missiles in its vicinity during the height of the Cold War. Because of an interest in both audio and video, project planners decided to do most of the interviews in a public studio or an adjoining room in the city library. One narrator did not want the studio setting and would only be interviewed at home. The same topics and themes were covered in all the interviews and the choices about who was to be interviewed in which setting at the studio were based primarily on the availability of the narrators, although one person specifically did not want to be interviewed on camera at the library. The interviews held in the studio with the interviewer and the camera operator resulted in repeated recountings of the

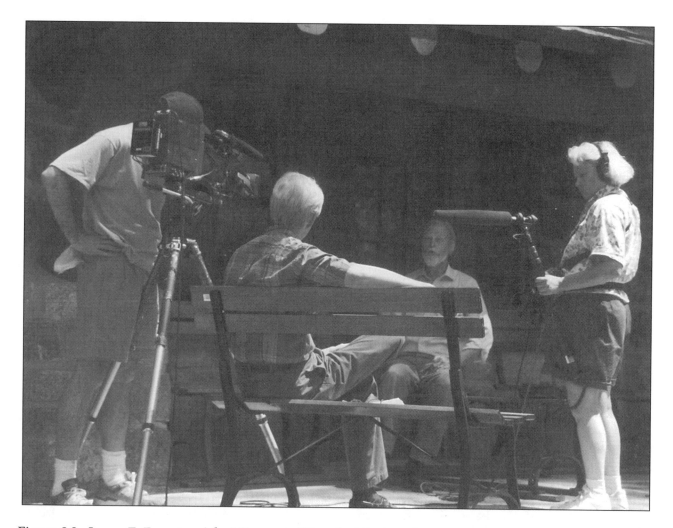

Figure 8.2. James E. Fogerty of the Minnesota Historical Society doing a video interview for the Minnesota Resort Industry Oral History Project. Note the position of the interviewer, narrator, camera operator, and the sound person holding the boom microphone. This project includes sixteen audio interviews and six follow-up video interviews. *Photo credit: Minnesota Historical Society.*

more public side of the story expressing support for the missile installations, while the interviews in the adjoining room, in which there was no video and only the interviewer and narrator were present, produced a more private side of the story including, in the case of the narrator who did not want to be on camera, fears about the future. The interview in the home resulted in a discussion of information the narrator would not have talked about in the more public setting, including active resistance to the missiles. The use of video is only one of several variables at work here and there are always additional factors to be considered. But this situation illustrates that the context in which the interview takes place is an important element affecting the interview's content and character.

The setting of an oral history interview is an integral part of the interview process. Visual settings can be expensive props or invaluable assets for enhancing the interview. As with all other parts of the oral history process, careful planning will add to the overall quality of the final product.

Notes

1. Brad Jolly, *Videotaping Oral History* (Nashville: American Association for State and Local History, 1982); "Tips for Better Interviewing," by Mark Gandolfo (n.d.).

CHAPTER 9

The Interview

What are good interviewing techniques? The interview is the most visible part of the oral history project. Good interviewing techniques are integral to its success. In this chapter we suggest a model for conducting an oral history interview, then review additional techniques.

After you have organized the interview setting, you will want to ask the narrator if he or she has any questions before the interview begins. This is a good time to review the language in the donor form and to let the narrator know he or she will be asked to sign it as soon as the interview is over. Some interviewers also take this time to ask the narrator to fill out a biographical information form to keep a record of the person's name, address, and other particulars. (A sample biographical information form is in appendix 2.) If using tape, always make sure the leader, or blank beginning few inches, has moved past the recording heads. Sound does not record on a leader, so advancing past it will ensure the interview is fully recorded. If more than one tape or disc is used, identifying information for each side and each additional tape should include name of interviewer, name of narrator, name of project, and date of interview.

After an equipment sound check, the interviewer will want to begin with a recorded introduction, such as:

The following interview was conducted with _____ (name of narrator) on behalf of the _____ for the _____ Oral History Project. It took place on _____ (date) at _____ (place). The interviewer is _____ (name).

Additional descriptive information may be given, but is not necessary. The introduction should be brief, to the point, and thorough. Adding too much information about the expected interview topics could give the impression that the interviewer is not interested in information on other topics that, when brought up, could lead to interesting, important, new, and pertinent information.

As a rule of thumb, the interview should unfold in chronological order and generally should be

The interviewer should always put an introduction on the tape or disc before starting the interview. This should include:

- name of narrator
- name of interviewer
- place of interview
- date of interview
- name of oral history project
- name of repository
- tape number (if more than one tape is used during the interview).

This is usually done in the interview setting and is a signal to the narrator that the interview is ready to begin. Several additional minutes may be left blank at the beginning of the first tape if the interviewer wishes to add summary information about the content of the interview after it has been completed.

structured to elicit both facts about the time, place, or event that is the focus of the interview as well as the narrator's thoughts about and analysis of the facts. Even if an interview focuses on a specific subject or event, the interviewer should begin with questions about personal background. This should be brief, but is a good way to start virtually every interview because the questions are easy for the narrator to answer and it provides a context for evaluating subsequent information the narrator gives. Some interviewers have found that initial questions about a narrator's work experience prove useful in getting a reticent narrator to relax, open up, and talk freely about past experiences.

After these background questions, move to the interview topics, beginning with when, how, and why the narrator initially became involved with the subject or event. This sets the stage for the narrator to tell the story from the beginning. Then move to questions about the subject or event. Prompted by open-ended questions, the narrator will talk about what happened, what he or she did or observed,

Interviewing Tips

Use open-ended questions. Tell me about . . . Describe . . .

Don't be judgmental or let your own opinions show. The interview is the narrator's time to tell his or her story.

Use your background research to prompt the narrator as necessary. Reminders of names, dates, places, and events are helpful.

Ask about thoughts and feelings. It is the subjective information that helps make oral history such an interesting primary source.

Don't interrupt the narrator. Wait until he or she is finished to ask another question.

Be prepared to ask follow-up questions to clarify information.

Don't argue with the narrator's information. If you question its accuracy, politely ask the narrator for greater elaboration. You may find the narrator's story actually sets the written record straight.

Be thoroughly familiar with the research and the topics you intend to pursue. It breaks the rhythm of the interview to be constantly referring to the interview outline or to other notes.

Know how to operate the recording equipment. Practice repeatedly before the interview and always do a sound check before beginning.

Thank the narrator when finished. Follow this with a written thank you letter.

terview, for it helps enrich understanding of the past by looking at events or actions from different perspectives. Narrators also will sometimes contradict themselves, and if they do, interviewers should strive for clarification by gently calling attention to the apparent contradictions. Sometimes it will turn out that a narrator simply misspoke. But in other cases, a narrator's response can offer fascinating insights into how the person tries to reconstruct and make sense of the past—one of the multiple layers of meaning that can be embedded in an oral history interview.

Finally, ask the narrator to assess the experience or event. Why did things happen as they did? What did the narrator think about it then? What does he or she think about it now? Asking for the narrator's analysis and reflections obtains insight into his or her thinking, another important aspect of oral history. Pragmatically, it also signals the interview is winding down and provides for a graceful closing.[1]

Interviewers working with one person on a series of life interviews will follow the same process of beginning with questions that are easy for the narrator to answer, then moving to the subject of the interview, and finally assessing the information as the interview winds down. Life interviews are often organized around specific periods in the person's life. This gives each interview session a focus for both interviewer and narrator.

Oral history interviews generally last from one-and-a-half to two hours. An interview of three hours or longer often ends with extreme narrator and interviewer fatigue. If you think you'll need extensive information from one narrator, plan for more than one interview session. Keep track of the time during an interview, making sure not to tire out the narrator before covering key points. Judging how much time to spend on personal questions at the beginning and on questions that set up the body of the interview is the interviewer's responsibility and should be carefully considered and thoughtfully addressed.

A list of guidelines for interviewers should include the following:

and what others did. After listening to the narrator's account, a thoroughly prepared interviewer will be able to explore the information further and attempt to clarify any apparent contradictions with other written or spoken accounts. Understanding contradictions, not resolving them, is the point of the in-

- Always keep the ethics of the situation in mind. An oral history interview is not a casual two-way conversation, a social call, or a heated debate over the interpretation of the past. Narrators are entitled to respect for their stories.

- Rely on open-ended questions. They elicit the most information. Examples are: "What were you told?" "How did you celebrate Christmas?" "Tell me about . . ." "Describe . . ."

- Use neutral, not leading, questions. Asking the narrator "Why don't you like living here?" will not result in as complete an answer as the more neutral question, "Tell me about living here." Questions beginning with *how, what, when, why, where,* and *who* are often used to introduce a subject or to follow up an initial statement. They can help clarify an answer and can elicit further information.

- Ask only one question at a time, not a smorgasbord of questions that will puzzle the narrator. If clarification is needed, make sure your elaboration does not lead the narrator to believe you expect a particular type of answer.

- Always remain neutral. Your opinions on the subject are not the focus of the interview.

- Remember you are there to collect the narrator's story, not to tell your own. Keep your focus on the narrator and don't show off your knowledge.

- Listen carefully without interrupting the narrator. The goal in an oral history interview is to collect long answers from well-focused, clearly stated, open-ended, neutral questions, although you should be aware there may be cultural variations that affect this pattern.

- If the narrator insists on telling a rehearsed story, listen politely and let him or her finish. Then go back and ask additional questions.

- Concentrate on what the narrator is saying. Wait until he or she has finished speaking to ask follow-up questions for clarification or to develop new information that did not emerge in the research process.

- Watch for hints, such as pauses or slight changes in voice, that indicate the narrator may have additional thoughts or feelings to describe and ask respectful follow-up questions.

- Use information identified through background and narrator-specific research to help facilitate a smooth interview. This may be as simple as supplying the correct date for an event or the name of someone connected with the event. Providing such information saves the narrator the frustration of trying to remember specifics or the possible embarrassment of giving incorrect information. It also indicates the project is important enough to have interviewers who are thoroughly prepared.

- It helps to ask the narrator to put an event or memory into the context of time and place as much as possible. This may be done by encouraging the narrator to think in terms of people and places that have ties to the interview topics. For example, one narrator, when asked to think about a specific subject in this way, closed his eyes and asked the interviewer what year he should put himself back to. This helped him put the memory into context. Another technique is to ask the narrator to describe what a place or event from the past looked like.

- Use the list of names and dates as necessary to help the narrator put events in context. Photographs, maps, and drawings are also useful aids, although careful verbal descriptions of each will have to be given in audio interviews.

- Remember to ask for specifics of place names, names of people, and dates or context. Sometimes the narrator's story is so interesting you can forget to ask for these details.

- Try to establish where the narrator was and what his or her connection to the story was at each major point. This will help differentiate firsthand information from reports given by others.

- Avoid asking questions beyond the narrator's expertise or about things he or she will not know firsthand.

- When a narrator uses acronyms or jargon that the general public is unfamiliar with, ask for explanations, descriptions, spellings, or translations, as appropriate. Your research or specific knowledge may mean you understand what the narrator is saying, but others listening to the interview or reading the transcript will probably not share this knowledge.

- Use body language and eye contact to encourage the narrator's responses. Smiles and nods are often effective. Silence is also an effective tool to elicit information. Repeated verbal encouragement by the interviewer, such as "uh-huhs," are intrusive and lower the sound quality of the interview.

- Discourage requests to turn off the recorder at any time during the interview. Only information given during the recorded interview will become part of the historical record. You may choose to put the recorder on "pause" to clarify something for the narrator. This can usually be done in a way that will not affect the rhythm of the interview. You will have to be prepared to make these decisions on the spot.

- Take breaks. This can be done when a cassette or disc is changed (or when an analog tape is turned over). Allow time to stretch, leave the room, get a drink of water, or quickly review the topics to be covered in the next part of the interview.

- Observe the narrator's body language. He or she may be uncomfortable with a line of questioning, want to take a break, or become tired. Be sensitive to the situation and handle it appropriately.

- Use a notebook to keep a running list of proper names mentioned in the interview. It is a good idea to ask the narrator to review this list and correct any spelling errors at the end of the interview. This list should be kept in the master file, with a copy given to the processor.

- Use a notebook to keep track of follow-up questions, additional points to make, or other interview needs. This will help keep you organized and will allow you to continue to concentrate on the narrator.

- Keep track of the time to make sure you don't extend the interview past a reasonable limit.

- Immediately label each tape or disc. This should include the oral history project name, the name of the narrator, the name of the interviewer, the date, and the tape number (for example, 1 of 3 generated in the interview).

- Take a black-and-white photograph of the narrator in the interview setting. This should be done for both audio and video interviews.

- Sign the donor form with the narrator, even if you plan more sessions with him or her.

Narrators sometimes will not immediately give long answers to questions. In such cases, it helps to wait before asking the next question, making sure he or she is not considering an additional comment. If nothing is forthcoming, you may have to realize the narrator is not interested in or comfortable with the question and switch to a different topic or approach.

As the interview progresses, the narrator, understanding the direction of the questions, may anticipate several points on the interview outline and cover them with one answer. You will want to be prepared with follow-up questions if necessary. Or, if the information is complete, move to another subject.

Some people habitually answer with short sentences or one or two words. You should try to ask questions that elicit as much information as possible, but should remember that each narrator is unique and treat the situation respectfully. You should verbally interpret nonverbal responses, especially in audio interviews. A brief "I see that you nodded yes to my question," will help clarify the situation.

On the other hand, some narrators talk a great deal. A good interviewer is prepared to keep the interview focused on the topics at hand in a polite and gentle manner. Although it is generally better to avoid unnecessarily interrupting, interviewers should be prepared to ask a question at an appropriate moment, such as when the narrator changes the subject.

At times, an interviewer may arrive as scheduled only to discover that the narrator has changed his or her mind about participating for any of a variety of reasons—the narrator's health is not good, the time scheduled for the interview is not good, the narrator is unexpectedly busy, the health of family members is not good, and the like. Interviewers should be able to review the situation and come up with a solution, which may be as easy as rescheduling.

Narrators also might be unwilling to be interviewed for a variety of other reasons. The topics to be covered, while important to the project, may be irritating or difficult for the narrator to discuss. In some cases, talking about past events or people to whom the narrator was close can bring about emotional reactions. Be prepared for these eventualities. Oral history interviews, while sometimes difficult, offer the narrator a chance to tell fully his or her story and to contribute information about people important to him or her. Often, allowing the narrator a moment of silence or sadness before moving on to happier memories allows you to successfully complete the interview.

How an interviewer handles such emotional situations—whatever their cause—depends to a great extent upon the interviewer's own interpersonal skills and ability to deal with his or her own emotional responses to difficult topics. Candor coupled with dedication to the purposes of the project—backed by thorough research and preparation for the interview—go a long way toward easing any discomfort a narrator and interviewer may experience.

Here's how one such situation unfolded. A young white woman in a small, Midwestern city eagerly sought to interview an elderly black woman, the granddaughter of slaves, as part of a fledgling community African-American history project. The interviewer and narrator were acquainted with one another, but the first time they recorded a formal oral history interview, it became clear that topics having to do with racial issues were difficult for them to discuss. When telling a story about her grandmother's childhood, for example, the elderly woman said: "Well, I'll skip that." Likewise, the interviewer passed up opportunities to ask follow-up questions about the elderly woman's schooling, jobs, relationships with young people of other races, episodes in the community involving the Ku Klux Klan, and so forth.

After critiquing the first interview, the young interviewer came to terms with her own discomfort in talking about race with an elderly woman whom she deeply respected. She wrote an introduction to the next interview, and recorded it at the beginning of their next session, in which she stressed the unique contribution the elderly woman could make by being willing and able to tell about what it was like to be a young African-American girl growing up in this small Midwestern city in the early 1900s.

The community and the state, the interviewer said,

> is extremely lucky to be able to listen to you and have a record of this part of the state's history, which was entrenched with institutional racism. You can teach us what it was like, and we can put together a document for others to learn from and gain a better understanding of what it was like for you to grow up here.

Then she described frankly, and on the record, the differences between them and the impact that might have on their interview:

> It is hard to talk about racial issues sometimes. It may be difficult for me to ask you certain questions, and difficult for you to answer, but I hope we can try. It may be easier for you to talk about the racism you encountered or observed with another African-American woman. I can try to set that up . . . but right now I am available and would like to see what you and I can accomplish. A few positive things you and I have together is that we know each other, trust each other, and respect each other. We are both women that like to talk about our lives, and we are friends.

The result? Greater candor by the elderly narrator about subtle and overt forms of racism in the community and more willingness by the narrator to ask questions about a concealed past.

On another occasion as the relationship between the two women evolved, two women friends of the elderly narrator came to visit her as the interviewer was leaving. The narrator had told a story that day about a friend who wanted to get out of the hospital so she could go home and cook herself some meat. She repeated the story to the two visitors, but in that version, the friend couldn't wait to get home to cook herself up some turnip greens and ham hocks.

"At first I was a little hurt," the interviewer recalled. "But after going over it and over it in my mind, I realize that she probably just didn't think I'd get it. Or more likely, that I just wouldn't appreciate it."

This episode illustrates the layers of complexity an oral history interview can reveal. Plans call for a young African-American woman to interview the granddaughter of slaves, and the resulting interview will almost certainly reveal insights into racial issues that only an exchange between two African-American women could uncover. Collectively, the interviews will enrich not only our understanding of the narrator's experience but also our understanding of how she interprets that experience for others. The episode also serves to illustrate that oral history is not a natural science. It is an intense interaction between two people. And those people can never stop being who they are—men or women, black or white, young or old. Each combination of narrator and interviewer results in a unique oral history interview. And that's why it's important to document fully all the variables that might affect future users' interpretations of the interview.

The importance of asking open-ended questions cannot be overemphasized. As Don Ritchie pointed out in his book *Doing Oral History*, open-ended questions allow narrators "to volunteer their own accounts, speculate on matters, and have enough time to include all the material they think relevant to the subject." He added that open-ended questions also "empower" narrators, shifting the balance of power from the interviewer to the narrator. Through this, the narrator can "control the situation, shaping the interview rather than just passively responding to questions."[2]

Sometimes narrators may indicate their feelings about subjects being discussed through body language. These are nonverbal responses to questions, such as pointing a finger, leaning toward the interviewer, leaning away from the interviewer, crossing the arms and legs, shifting or moving noticeably, breaking eye contact, and talking slower or faster than normal. You will want to be aware of these clues and respond to them as necessary. It is sometimes helpful to respectfully mention a nonverbal response and ask the narrator to discuss his or her feelings in more depth.

Project coordinators should try to pair narrators with interviewers to whom they will respond best. This usually means not pairing people who know each other well or with whom they have had a long association. An oral history interview between two old friends often results in "insider" information that others may not understand.

It is usually best to interview one person at a time and to have as few people in the room as possible during an interview. An interview is an intense situation because of the degree of concentration required by both the interviewer and the narrator, and narrators tend to be more comfortable with fewer people around, although some cultures may require or encourage witnesses or observers.

If you are interested in interviewing several people together, you will want to consider using video. However, you will want to think carefully about what this interview will produce. Despite the ideal give-and-take several people in a group seems to offer, what generally happens is that one person dominates or the narrators contradict one another enough to bog down the interview. It takes an experienced interviewer to keep an interview with multiple narrators moving along effectively.

Ending an interview is an art in itself. Oral history interviews are intense and can involve revelation of extremely personal information. To help the narrator wind down, the interviewer might ask a few introspective questions while giving the narrator an opportunity to add any thoughts or information that might not have been covered elsewhere.

After signing the donor form, the interviewer may want to sit and talk for a little while to help the narrator unwind. This often depends on how tired the narrator is and the interviewer's schedule. This is the time to ask the narrator exactly how to record his or her name on project files. Sometimes, this is the time for the coffee or tea you couldn't accept during the interview. A measured packing up of interview equipment also allows for after-interview comments and discussion. Another good end-of-interview activity is to review the spelling of proper names jotted down during the interview. While a good exercise for interviewer and narrator, it also provides helpful information for people processing the interview. If this isn't done at the end of the interview, you will want to call the narrator as soon as possible to review and check this information.

Narrators often have photos, other archival material, or artifacts related to the information discussed. If so, they may want either to give the items to the repository holding the oral history project or to loan them for copying (especially in the case of photographs). If project planning calls for taking this information at the time of the interview, you should carefully inventory all materials, signing and giving one copy of the inventory to the narrator while keeping the other with interview records. If the information is to be identified for future consideration, the interviewer will still want to look it over and be able to write a description for project coordinators.

Sometimes, during discussions after the interview, a narrator remembers something pertinent to the interview. If possible, you should try to record this information, even if it means unpacking the recorder and setting it up again. As an alternative to this, you can take thorough notes and ask the narrator to schedule another interview session.

Finally, be prepared to answer any questions the narrator might have about the project repository, accessibility, and future use of the interview. If full transcription is to be done, let the narrator know he or she will be sent a copy to review and correct before it is put into final form. It is also a good idea to offer the narrator a personal copy of the interview cassettes or discs, explaining when they will be sent.

You may find you need to conduct an interview by telephone. This should be done with care and planning and only if necessary. Time restrictions that can result in forcing the interview to move at too fast a pace, lack of personal rapport, and the inability to read body language and other signs important to an interviewer are all concerns that will have to be carefully addressed if plans call for a telephone interview.

The guidelines for interviewing apply equally to audio and video. However, several additional techniques should be considered with video. A video interview is not a polished documentary program ready for use on television. It is a video version of an audio interview. As such, its focus is on collecting the information as the narrator tells it. Although the video adds a more formal touch to the process, narrator and interviewer should not feel constrained by the presence of the camera. The narrator should be free to start and stop talking in a relaxed manner, including false starts. Do not abandon the use of silences or pauses, though they are more noticeable because of the camera.

More time constraints affect the use of video, either in a studio or on-site, than audio. It can be easier for the audio interviewer to go a little beyond the allotted one or one-and-a-half hours if the situation calls for it, while camera and studio time are usually rented by the hour and may be tightly scheduled. Because of this, the interviewer should keep an even closer eye on the time during a video interview, making sure to cover the most important or critical information first. Video interviews conducted outside a studio may allow the same flexibility as an audio-only interview. If a narrator has photographs or other material pertinent to the interview, the videographer may be asked to film this material, accompanied by the narrator's description of each item.

Narrator and interviewer must sign the donor form after all interviews, regardless of whether they are in audio (including telephone) or video format. As stated in chapter 3, federal copyright law specifies that the words on the tape are protected by copyright and may not be used without the person's permission.

Send a thank-you letter to the narrator as soon as possible after the interview. It should thank the person for his or her time and reinforce the importance of the information given. See the sample in appendix 3.

Although there is no substitute for thorough research and careful preparation before conducting oral history interviews, we offer this caveat: Be prepared to be flexible.

Retired Arlington County, Virginia, librarian Sara Collins recalled an occasion where an elderly woman came to Arlington on a "last" trip to her hometown and wanted to visit the school she'd attended from 1913 to 1915. Collins opened the building, which had since become the Arlington Historical Museum, and the interviewer from the library's oral history program rushed over, recorder in hand. The result was a priceless account of the woman's school days, in which she recalled the arrangement of classrooms, described the daily routine of fetching coal and water, and talked about teachers and classmates she remembered. Flexibility and an experienced interviewer combined with a willing, articulate narrator to capture an unplanned, firsthand account of a long-ago era.

Oral history interviews are as unique as the people who give them. Each will represent the narrator and his or her characteristics. As such, interviewing techniques will vary with each interview. A well-prepared interviewer, however, can elicit much information important to the overall project. It is not always easy. The interview can be an intense experience for both interviewer and narrator, but the results are well worth the effort.

Notes

1. The above description of a model interview format is based on the teaching of Martha Ross, retired from the University of Maryland and past Oral History Association president.

2. Donald A. Ritchie, *Doing Oral History* (New York: Twayne Publishers, 1995), 67.

CHAPTER 10

Processing and Care

What do you do when the interview is over? The interview is an exciting part of the oral history process, but good processing and care techniques afterward ensure the information in it will be available to more people than just the interviewer.

The first processing step is to clearly label the cassettes or discs with the name of narrator, interviewer, oral history project, date, and number (i.e., cassette or disc 1, 2, and so on from the interview). Next, pop the tabs on the top of audio or videocassettes to protect the material on the tapes. This will, in most cases, prevent re-recording over the preservation masters. Copy the cassettes or discs as soon as possible after the interview to prevent loss or destruction of information on them. If no other audio exists, the audio portion of video footage also should be immediately copied as back-up. This is also the time to check for the possibility, however remote, of potentially defamatory statements in the interview. If found, take the steps described in chapter 3. After you have done this, deposit the interview masters in the repository and distribute copies to the processor. Depending on the situation, you may also want to give a copy to the narrator at this time.

Ideally, you should strive for full verbatim, subject-indexed transcripts of all interviews (both audio and video). These are the most useful for researchers who can then quickly locate material in which they are interested. But they are also time consuming and expensive to create, requiring eight to twelve hours of processing time for each interview hour. Machines or computers with headphone and foot pedal attachments are the most efficient way to transcribe; transcribing machines that use full-size analog cassettes can be helpful. Video interviews are often also recorded in audio, which aids transcribing.

If your project elects to transcribe the interviews, try to work with someone skilled at translating the spoken word to the written page. The subtleties of sentence structure, paragraph development, and punctuation can be difficult to determine, and incorrect representations can result in misleading or incorrect interpretation of the information. Following are standard transcribing guidelines:

> **Transcribing Suggestions**
>
> It is helpful to put a time code in the left margin of the transcript. This will help readers find the spoken quote to listen to.
>
> Transcribe every word in the order spoken by the narrator, leaving out only the "ums" and "ahs."
>
> Check with project coordinators on how to handle slang expressions, such as "yeah." Some want it kept, others prefer it be changed to "yes."
>
> Make sure you spell all words accurately. Check the spelling of all proper and place names carefully to insure they are correct.
>
> Add full names and titles as necessary in brackets the first time a name is mentioned. Example: [Senator John] Doe.
>
> Listen carefully. If you can't understand a word or phrase after checking it three times, indicate this on the transcript. Check with the interviewer about missing words or phrases. Sometimes the interviewer or the narrator can fill in the missing information.

- A transcript should begin with a heading identifying the oral history project name, the name of the narrator, the name of the interviewer, and the date and place of the interview. Below this, indicate the abbreviations that will be used to identify each speaker. This may be done using the person's initials (see examples in appendix) or by using Q and A for question and answer. Each new tape or disc should be identified with an internal heading (Tape One, Side One).

- Transcripts should be paginated and double-spaced, including changes from interviewer to narrator. This is especially true for review copies and drafts for ease in inserting necessary comments and corrections.

- Do not indent.

- Determine a stylistic approach regarding use of paragraphs. Some oral historians prefer a person's comments be presented in one long paragraph, regardless of change in subjects. Others prefer that an extremely long statement be broken into shorter blocks for ease of reading.

- A transcript should be as accurate a representation of the interview as possible. It should include false starts (which can indicate thought process), Freudian slips, abrupt changes in subject, and grammatical errors. All help to accurately represent the interview. Some oral historians instruct transcribers to delete repetitive *and/and so* at the beginning of sentences and *ums* and *ahs* when they occur, but little else should be omitted.

- Even a well-done interview can sometimes yield indecipherable words. In these cases, after working as carefully as possible to figure out the words (rewinding and listening to the spot several times), the transcribers should mark the spot with (_____???) to indicate the need to fill in a word or phrase. Questions about the spelling of a specific word should also be noted—(??). Mark phonetic spellings with (ph).

- Abbreviations should never be used except for common titles (e.g., Mrs., Dr.). Never use the ampersand (&); spell out the word. Also, the numbers one through nine should be spelled out, while 10 and higher should be represented with numerals. The same rule applies for first through ninth and 10th and higher.

- Use brackets to insert explanatory information. For instance, abbreviations and acronyms should be spelled out the first time the term is mentioned. Examples: USGS [United States Geological Survey], SAC [Strategic Air Command]. Specific descriptions should be included, such as [laughs], [pounds table], [phone rings] and nonverbal spoken

sounds [pffft] should be indicated. The transcript should note any time the recorder was turned off and any mechanical failings with a brief statement. Example: [noise from jet landing at nearby airport interrupted interview].

- Include the full name of a person when mentioned for the first time. If the narrator mentions only a first or last name, the transcriber should fill in the full name [John] Doe. When a community is mentioned, the name of the state should be included in brackets, such as Worthington [Minnesota].

- Use footnotes, both explanatory and reference, wherever necessary. Explanatory footnotes provide additional information about a statement. Example: If a narrator mentions a specific event that is important to the interview, additional information can be given in a short explanatory footnote to help put the statement into context. References should be included for information about publications or other materials mentioned during the interview. Example: If a narrator mentions a publication, the full citation should be given in a footnote.

- Narrators often quote others during an interview. Enclose all quotes in quotation marks. Transcribers will have to determine punctuation needs, such as where to insert commas, ellipses, and dashes. Standard writing style guides govern the use of commas. Transcribers may be tempted to insert commas whenever a person pauses, but commas should be used only when called for under customary rules of grammar and punctuation.

- Generally, ellipses are used to indicate an incomplete sentence (Then we went . . .), while dashes indicate a change in thought in mid-sentence (Then we went—he went—we all went to the theater).

- Projects will want to determine at the outset how to handle such things as persistent mispronunciations, grammatical errors, vernacular speech, and regional speech patterns. Most try to reflect the interview as accurately as possible, but this is a decision that should be carefully and thoroughly thought out. Attempts to replicate dialect on paper can be seen as pejorative.

- Transcribers will learn a narrator's speech patterns and where breaks or pauses in sentences or thoughts occur. Often, when people begin speaking after pausing, their voices pick up as they would at the beginning of a new sentence. Transcribers should be aware of such situations and know how to listen to determine when to continue a sentence and when to start a new one.

Transcribing involves listening carefully to each word in the interview. This is intense work and can be tiring. The possibility of making mistakes or mishearing words or phrases increases as the ability to concentrate decreases; it is important to take regular breaks when transcribing.

Transcripts are helpful tools in maintaining access to the interviews. They can also improve access to the physical recordings. Including time code indicators on the transcript ties them to the recorded interview and helps someone locate a specific quote. For audio, this involves listening to the interview while either reading and timing the transcript or reading it while checking the time codes on the tape or disc. The transcriber then inserts the elapsed time or time code at regular intervals in the left margin of the transcript. For video, this is a two-step process. The first is to develop a transcript, most easily done using an audio copy of the interview. The transcriber then inserts the time codes on the transcript by viewing the video while reading the transcript, noting time codes from the videotape in the left-hand margin. The time code will look like 01:01:05:30, the numbers indicating hour, minute, second, and frame number. Enter the hour, minute, and second numbers at the beginning, at approximately three-minute intervals throughout the transcript, and at the end. Examples are included in appendix 6.

After a draft of the interview is completed, audit-check it for accuracy. This involves carefully listening to the interview while reading along on the transcript, marking all necessary corrections. An audit-check helps catch spelling errors, omitted words, misinterpreted words or phrases, obvious misspeaking of dates or names by interviewer or narrator, and errors that can occur when the transcriber misinterprets a pause or break in speaking. It is often necessary to listen to a sentence or a phrase several times to make sure it has been correctly transcribed. Corrections should be made with red ink or pencil if possible, and should be cleanly printed above the corrected spot or in the page margin with a marked indicator to the location of the correction (fig. 10.1).

After the audit-check is completed and marked corrections have been made, many oral history projects send a clean copy of the updated draft to the narrator for further review. Narrators can help in the transcription process; by reviewing the document, they can catch inaccuracies in translating the spoken to the written word as well as check for correct spelling of all proper names mentioned. When narrators are asked to review the interview transcript, however, it helps to remind them that a transcript of spoken words will not read like a written document. It can seem choppy and, at times, appear repetitious. Narrators should resist the urge to thoroughly edit it; the goal is to have a clean, accurate document that resembles as closely as possible the spoken original. See example in appendix 6.

Narrator review should not be skipped if narrators have limited eyesight or difficulty reading. In those situations, either the interviewer or the transcriber should take the draft transcript to the narrator and slowly read it through, allowing the narrator to indicate necessary corrections.

Keep a copy of the corrected draft in the narrator's master file at the repository. This will help future users of the information to understand any minor differences between the spoken and written words.

When all corrections have been made and you have a clean, corrected copy of the transcript, develop an index. This can include proper and place names or be expanded to include interview topics. The index can be created by the word processing program used in transcription. If this option is used, the program marks the item to be included in the index with a character that does not print out on the final document, but which identifies the word as an index item and then follows it to keep the page number listing accurate. Some projects take indexing a step further by compiling individual indexes into a cumulative index covering all project interviews.

Finally, create a title page, identifying narrator, name of project, date of interview, and interviewer. With this, you have created an oral history transcript. An example of a transcript and a sample title page are included in appendix 6. Make a copy of

Sample Page, Audit-Edited Transcript

0.10

JB: ~~They~~ *And,* said, "Oh, it was the best grant we had ever seen," so we felt good, *about that,* even

though they didn't fund it because it was about women. We just put it in again. We were

funded for three years. I will say that writing the grant was a huge experience. It was a

big, federal project, *Kind of* funneled through the state.

LW: Who told you that you had received the federal grant after the second *time* ~~submission~~?

0.12

JB: People at the state department *[of education]* because, I believe, they *actually* decided who got the money

after they had an overall block grant. There might have been some restrictions on that, *too.*

The upshot was that we finally were funded. I can remember us *[my co-leader and I]* going to a workshop on

how to do these grants and coming out of it and looking at each other, saying, "Did you

understand any of that?" All that jargon that you *sort of* take for granted after a while.

0.15

So, we were funded. We got going in a tiny little office over in Center City High School.
[from teaching at West City because of student population decline]
It was wonderful for me because I was laid off, about that time. But West City continued

to fund the project. There was always money that had to come from each school district

as well as federal grant money. They continued to give us support as far as the teachers

and the matching funds. That was a *three* ~~five~~-year project and was the beginning of our

international women's studies project.

Figure 10.1. A page from a transcript showing audit-editing marks.

the subject-indexed transcript and the title page on acid-free paper (lignin-free and alkaline with a pH greater than 7) for deposit with the interview masters at the repository. Many projects also send a completed copy to the narrator and make and bind a copy for public use at the repository.

If limited finances preclude transcribing, develop a tape log with a full abstract. One version, called TAPE (Time Access to Pertinent Excerpts) is a time-coded log of information in the interview.[1] To develop an abstract, listen to the interview and write a clear, concise, accurate, and detailed one- or two-page summary. This will help future researchers understand what is in the interview and assess its contents. Then, listening to the interview again and using a stopwatch if necessary, record time elapsed as each new subject is discussed. Both abstract and tape log should contain a complete and correctly spelled list of all proper names mentioned in the interview. With only a tape log, ongoing access to information in the interview depends on availability of equipment to play the tape or disc. An example is included in appendix 6.

In an attempt to ease initial transcription work, some oral historians have experimented with computer-based voice recognition systems. Currently, these systems are incapable of differentiating among voices in the interview or responding to the subtle needs of sentence structure, paragraph development, and full punctuation. People interested in further information about these systems should contact audio-visual archivists at their state historical societies or the Oral History Association.

As you begin to turn the materials over to the repository, check the storage area if you can and look for details. You will want to know about storage conditions for the transcript and for the tapes or discs. Is the interview information protected by storing the transcripts in a separate area from the recordings? Are the storage areas clean? Is the temperature and humidity in a range of 70 degrees Fahrenheit and 50 percent humidity? Are humidity and temperature levels stable? Are patrons allowed to remove items from shelves and check them out and, if so, what are the procedures to maintain con-

trol over the collections? What procedures are in place to prevent loss and damage and to protect from theft? The project repository will have standard specifications for optimum care and maintenance.

Cassettes and discs will last longer if kept in archival containers under relatively constant temperature and humidity. It is best to avoid extreme heat and cold, excessive moisture, dust, and atmospheric pollutants. Use metal shelving if possible and seal wooden shelves against acidity. Avoid particle board shelves. The repository should keep an acid-free paper copy of the subject-indexed transcript or abstract and tape log in an acid-free file folder as part of the narrator's master file, which should not circulate (be accessible to the public). The black-and-white photograph of the narrator in the interview setting, enclosed in an acid-free folder clearly labeled with the narrator's name, the date of the interview, and the project name, also should be kept in the file. Copies of the transcript should be made for use by researchers.

> Not all products labeled "acid-free" will be safe for you to use when caring for oral history materials. The term is not standardized and some commercial products, while technically free of acid when developed, may develop acids later. Check your sources carefully.

Interview processing and attention to care of the recordings, while admittedly time consuming and not the most glamorous parts of the oral history process, pay years of dividends. It ensures ongoing access to the information in the interview that so many labored so hard to create.

Notes

1. Dale Treleven, *TAPE (Time Access to Pertinent Excerpts) System: A Method for Producing Oral History Interviews and Other Sound Recordings* (Madison: State Historical Society of Wisconsin, 1979).

CHAPTER 11

Now What?

What's next? Completing an oral history project is fulfilling. The work has tapped the skills and expertise of many people, from interviewers and narrators to support staff and transcribers. Project coordinators sometimes celebrate with an open house or gathering, inviting all project participants. This may be the only time the processors actually meet the people whose words they worked with. It also offers interviewers a chance to see their narrators again. Such gatherings provide a fitting end to a project, commemorating the results and thanking all who helped make it possible. They also can be part of a project's planned publicity, for an oral history project should not hide its light under a bushel.

An important purpose of collecting oral history is to develop new primary source material and make it available to researchers. The information a project unearths often attracts attention because of its subject or the fact that it is new and exciting. And uses for the information abound, limited only by the imagination. They can include:

- Museum exhibits. (An entire museum on the history of the Civilian Conservation Corps was created in Chisholm, Minnesota, using interviews, photographs, and artifacts collected through a Minnesota oral history project. The Nebraska State Historical Society Museum in Lincoln has created exhibits titled "What Did You Do in the War?" based on a World War II project and "Our Treasures: A Celebration of Nebraska's Mexican Heritage," a bilingual exhibit based on an oral history project documenting the state's Mexican-American population.) (fig. 11.1)

- Written materials, including books, newspaper articles, and poetry. (The Prince William County, Virginia, Historical Commission sponsored a series of local newspaper articles, based largely on oral histories about communities in the county disappearing in the wake of developers' bulldozers. Andrew J. Dunar and Dennis McBride relied on oral histories in their book *Building Hoover Dam: An Oral History of the Great Depression*, just one of hundreds of titles that could be named, which draw in whole or in part on oral history interviews.)

- Performances, such as songs and theatrical presentations. (Lee Patton Chiles of the Historyonics Theatre Company created *Through the Eyes of a Child: Coming Home*, a one-act play based on the Missouri Historical Society's oral history research project focusing on African-American neighborhoods in St. Louis. Moises Kaufman's *The Laramie Project*, based on oral history interviews about the beating death of Matthew Shepherd in Laramie, Wyoming, is another example.)

- Public education programs. (Teacher Michael A. Brooks of Suva Intermediate School in Bell Gardens, California, created his "Long, Long Ago Oral History Project" more than twenty years ago. The ongoing project has involved students in every stage of carrying out an oral history project, from research to interviews to publications and other public presentations based on their work.)

- Identification and marking of historic sites. (The National Park Service has used oral history in work with Alaska natives to identify traditional native place names in wilderness areas. The park service relies extensively on oral history to enrich documentation and interpretation at numerous sites around the country.)

- Genealogy or family research.

- Internet Web site development. (Everyone with a computer and the willingness to tinker a bit with it seems eager to put oral history materials online, and Web sites have proliferated like bunny rabbits. One example of a first-rate site is the California State University Long Beach Virtual Oral/Aural History Project at www.csulb.edu/voaha.)

Figure 11.1. The Minnesota Civilian Conservation Corps History Building at Ironworld Discovery Center, Chisholm, Minnesota. All exhibits were developed from materials and information in the Minnesota Civilian Conservation Corps Documentation Project (oral history project) collections. Support was given by Chapter 119 of the National Association of CCC Alumni. *Photo credit: Iron Range Research Center, Ironworld Discovery Center, Chisholm, Minnesota.*

Oral history is a research tool that works across cultures and around the world. The Mille Lacs band of Ojibwe (Minnesota) people has used oral history for a number of years to record traditional stories told by the last generation of their members to speak Ojibwe as a first language. Combining standard oral history techniques with respect for culture, the interviewers record stories at the time of year and in settings in which they traditionally would have been told. They then translate the interviews into English, standardizing spellings of proper and place names in the process. In another example, retired Gallaudet University history professor John S. Schuchman used oral history across several languages and cultures to document experiences of deaf Hungarian Jews who survived the Nazi concentration camps in World War II.

Although we conceived this manual for general public use and do not address specific needs of teachers, it is important to note that countless teachers at all levels of education use oral history techniques or the products of oral history in their classrooms. Oral history allows students to participate in a unique, hands-on method of learning across the curriculum, where history, language arts, public speaking, even keyboarding and creative multimedia project development intersect.

And it's not just for high school and college classrooms. Fourth grade teacher Susan Venter at Cavett Elementary School in Lincoln, Nebraska, created an oral history project for her students studying Nebraska history. Following a day-long visit to a one-room country schoolhouse, the fourth graders planned and conducted oral history interviews with parents and grandparents who attended or taught in one-room schools, a dying remnant of the once-dominant educational system on the prairie. Social studies students in Bethlehem Middle School in Delmar, New York, have interviewed numerous older members of the community about life experiences in the Great Depression, World War II, the Vietnam War, and about their recollections of a host of other historic events, like the assassination of John F. Kennedy, the D-Day invasion, and the resignation of Richard Nixon (fig. 11.2).

Excellent resources, such as "Talking Gumbo: A Teacher's Guide to Using Oral History in the Classroom" by Pamela Dean, Toby Daspit, and Petra Munro, "Oral History Projects in the Classroom," by Linda P. Wood, the recent publication of the Oral History Association for teachers, and "Pathways: Discovering Your Connections to History," from the American Association for State and Local History (AASLH), are available for teachers who wish to use oral history in the classroom. Chapter 12 and the bibliography to this manual list these and other sources of information. State historical societies, school district personnel, the Oral History Association, and the Association of Oral History Educators also are excellent sources of information for

Figure 11.2. Cavett Elementary School student Kaitlyn Waller of Lincoln, Nebraska, interviewing her grandfather, Jack Waller of Holdrege, Nebraska, for her class's One-Room Schoolhouse Oral History Project. Created by fourth-grade teacher Susan Venter, the project documented the experiences of her students' parents and grandparents who attended or taught in one-room schools. *Photo credit: Barbara W. Sommer.*

teachers who want to incorporate oral history in their classrooms.

The uses of oral history are limitless. Just as historians examine and reexamine diaries, letters, and other written artifacts of the past, so, too, will oral histories offer a continuing source of fodder for those who seek to understand both the content and the context of past times and places and the perspectives of those who both acted and were acted upon.

The modern practice of oral history, which evolved more than a half-century ago, has become a research technique used worldwide to collect and preserve otherwise undocumented information, often from the historically voiceless. In addition to preserving information about past times and places, often highlighting day-to-day lives of ordinary people, oral history collections also offer insight into the meaning narrators attach to those times and to their participation in bygone events, thus contributing new variegated strands to historians' efforts to weave tapestries about the past (fig. 11.3).

Oral histories also can reveal subtle themes and insights that project planners never imagined. In one project, the union representing workers at a century-old manufacturing plant interviewed dozens of workers for a centennial oral history book. Interviewers largely were interested in asking questions aimed at eliciting descriptions of foundry work and other jobs that no longer existed. What they collected were intricate details of how technology and production had changed over the years. But as the men and women reflected on their years at the plant, even more valuable stories emerged about the meaning of work and the relationships they treasured. Viewed collectively, the interviews revealed layers of human interaction that went far beyond the project's original intent of documenting physical changes in the manufacturing operations. Project planners never intended to examine a multidimensional view of the nature of work and of the evolving relationships among employees—men and women, black and white—since before World War II. But that's what the interviews revealed. And they created a rich treasure trove for future scholars willing to mine their words.

Indeed, an oral history collection often will yield new themes to new users who read the transcripts or listen to the tapes with fresh eyes and ears—like a quilt that is far more than the sum of its small shapes. The quilt might begin as a reflection of its maker's vision, but the county fair judge who examines it might see something else, which, in turn, might vary from what the quilter's grandchild sees on a cold, lonely night. Likewise, oral historians who embark on a project for a specific, short-term purpose might be surprised to learn what a gold mine they've created for future historians who seek new insights into a specific time and place in the past. It's intangible. It's invaluable. And it's what makes oral history worth doing.

Figure 11.3. Barb Sommer with examples of oral history-based publications. *Photo credit: Beth Rickers, Worthington [MN] Daily Globe.*

CHAPTER 12

Oral History Resources

This chapter provides information about several national organizations dedicated to supporting oral history and state and local history. Many more professional associations of academic historians also touch on oral history, but the following organizations are the best places to start.

The Oral History Association is the major support organization for oral historians. It brings together people from many professions and disciplines who practice history and who share a common interest in oral history. It publishes the *Oral History Review*, the *Oral History Association Newsletter*, a pamphlet series on subjects of interest to oral historians, and sponsors an annual conference.

> Oral History Association
> Dickinson College
> P.O. Box 1773
> Carlisle, Pennsylvania 17013
> 717-245-1036
> 717-245-1046 (fax)
> OHA@dickinson.edu
> Oral History Association homepage:
> www.dickinson.edu/oha/

The Oral History Association homepage contains, among other things, information about joining the organization and links to state and regional oral history groups. You may find information about a state or regional organization in your area using this resource. You can also download a copy of the *Evaluation Guidelines* from the site (fig. 12.1).

If you don't see a state or regional organization listed for your area, you should contact the Oral History Association directly. It will have additional information about OHA members and activities near you.

You might also wish to subscribe to the oral history electronic discussion list, the H-ORALHIST. Topics vary widely and have included discussions of equipment, announcements of educational programs, and requests for assistance from novice oral history practitioners. There are no dues or fees. To subscribe, send an e-mail message to: listserv@ h-net.msu.edu with no subject and the following text: SUBSCRIBE. H-ORALHIST first name last name, affiliation

The main H-ORALHIST Web site is: www. h-net.msu.edu/~oralhist

The Association of Oral History Educators serves teachers interested in using oral history as a teaching tool. For more information, contact:

> Association of Oral History Educators
> P.O. Box 24
> Ellicott City, Maryland 21403
> 410-744-5565 (telephone and fax)
> AOHELanman@aol.com
> www.geocities.com/aohelanman/

You can also find out more about this organization through the Oral History Association.

The American Association for State and Local History is a nonprofit educational organization dedicated to advancing knowledge, understanding, and appreciation of local history in the United States and Canada. It sponsors an annual conference, confers prizes and awards for outstanding achievement, and supports an educational program. It publishes *History News*, the *Dispatch*, the "Technical Leaflet" series, and offers a membership online discussion list. Through its book series published by AltaMira Press (Walnut Creek, California), it offers dozens of books for local history and museum practitioners, including several dealing with oral history.

> American Association for
> State and Local History
> 1717 Church Street
> Nashville, Tennessee 37203-2991
> 615-320-3203
> 615-320-9013 (fax)
> www.aaslh.org

For information on resources in your area, contact your state historical society or archives. The best way to find them is to consult the *Directory of Historical Organizations in the United States and Canada, 15th Edition*. Created by the American Association for State and Local History and published by AltaMira Press, the directory includes information about some 13,000 state and local history groups in North America, including detailed information on how to contact them. The directory includes historical societies, historic houses, historical agencies,

ORAL HISTORY ASSOCIATION
Volume XXXV Number 4
Winter 2001

Oral History Emerges from Terrorist Attacks

Almost before the dust had settled following the Sept. 11 terrorist attacks on the World Trade Center in New York City and the Pentagon in Washington, D.C., oral historians were making plans to document the events many observers were calling a turning point in American history.

Speaking at an early-morning special session at the Oral History Association meeting in St. Louis, President Mary Marshall Clark called it critical to "cast the net as widely as possible" to collect impressions and experiences of people affected by the attacks "before public stories, public interpretations impinge on their story." Oral historians' efforts to document individual experiences can "create a space for people to have alternative views," she said.

Clark announced that the Columbia University Oral History Research Office, which she heads, and Columbia's Institute for Social and Economic Research and Policy have received a grant of approximately $50,000 from the National Science Foundation to begin interviews with as many people as possible who were directly or indirectly affected by the attacks.

Other schools and departments at Columbia, New York-area museums, including the New York Historical Society and the Skyscraper Museum, and local history groups around the country are part of the collaborative effort.

The project is called the September 11, 2001, Oral History Narrative and Memory Project.

Relying initially on experienced interviewers from public radio and television and other media, the project had interviewed 200 people by mid-November, Clark said.

They represented a wide range: small business owners, Mexicans (some documented, some not), Muslims, other Arab Americans, refugees and immigrants from Afghanistan and Pakistan, eyewitnesses, physicians, rescue workers, community college students, artists whose studios or exhibit spaces were affected, people who lost loved ones, firefighters, police, volunteers, priests, other clerics, teachers, principals, people from the New York financial district, writers and journalists.

Clark said the project particularly sought to interview people from communities where citizens and non citizens have been victims of discrimination or reprisals after the attacks.

(Continued on page 3)

Gateway Arch Creates Backdrop for 2001 OHA Meeting

In the shadow of St. Louis' symbolic Gateway Arch, some 400 community historians and scholars, including 110 newcomers, attended the 35th annual meeting of the Oral History Association Oct. 17-21.

With the theme "Bearing Public Witness: Documenting Memories of Struggle and Resistance," program co-chairs Leslie Brown, Anne Valk and Jessica Wiederhorn, created more than 90 panels, forums, workshops and plenary sessions, which, coincidentally, also painted the backdrop for conferees' discussions of the Sept. 11 terrorist attacks in New York and Washington, D.C.

Jacqueline K. Dace and John Wolford of the Missouri Historical Society scheduled an array of off-site tours and special events, including the annual Presidential Reception at the Missouri History Museum and a theatrical performance of "Through the Eyes of a Child: Coming Home," based on oral history interviews with residents of four historically-black St. Louis neighborhoods.

The OHA also presented awards for best use of oral history in a book and in non-print format and its newly named Martha Ross Teaching Award for distinguished precollegiate teaching.

The following pages of this **OHA Newsletter** offer a reporter's notebook sampling from the St. Louis meeting's intellectual smorgasbord.

Figure 12.1. The *Oral History Association Newsletter.*

history museums, historic sites, gardens, archives, genealogical societies, tribal museums, and corporate history museums.

The directory is available in libraries or from:

AltaMira Press
A Division of Rowman & Littlefield
    Publishers, Inc.
1630 North Main Street, #367
Walnut Creek, California 94596
www.altamirapress.com

The Society of American Archivists is the oldest and largest national archival preservation organization. It provides information and education regarding the identification, preservation, and use of historical records.

Society of American Archivists
527 S. Wells Street – 5th Floor
Chicago, Illinois 60607-3922
312-922-0140
www.archivists.org

Oral history helps make the past come alive and stay alive. By preserving the words and thoughts of eyewitnesses to and participants in events, it helps us all understand a little bit more about why and how they happened. It is an excellent outreach tool for organizations and communities and offers an interdisciplinary approach to educational projects. It can help us all learn from the past and from the people around us, and preserving the interviews for future generations is a gift everyone involved in a project can give.

We have outlined the steps of an oral history project in this manual. Although they may seem like a lot of work, some will be relatively quick and easy to accomplish. Others you will want to invest significant time in, realizing that time spent at the beginning of the project can save you countless hours at the end. Following all the steps will help you develop a strong project that will add new documentary evidence to the historical record.

Oral history is a fascinating field full of wonderful opportunities for you and your organization or community. We wish you success.

Mary Kay Quinlan
Barb Sommer

Oral History Project Planning Steps

✓ Identify key leaders and project personnel

✓ Name the project

✓ Write a mission statement

✓ Decide who will own project materials (project repository)

✓ Develop a project budget

✓ Find funding and other support sources

✓ Select a project advisory board

✓ Establish a project timeframe

✓ Establish record-keeping procedures

✓ Develop a publicity plan

✓ Train interviewers

✓ Determine the equipment to use

✓ Begin background research on the subject to be covered by the project

✓ Develop a list of names and dates related to project themes or topics

✓ List possible interview themes or topics

✓ Identify potential narrators and the themes or topics to cover with each

✓ Do interviewee-specific research

✓ Develop the interview guide

✓ Schedule the interview

✓ Do the interview

✓ Process interview materials and turn them over to the repository

Suggested Record-Keeping Materials

Donor Form: Transfers copyright of an oral history interview to the designated repository. Signed by both the narrator and the interviewer, and any other person whose voice is heard in the interview, as soon as the interview session ends even if more interviews are planned with the narrator.

Donor Form (Restricted Access): This form works the same as the donor form, except it restricts access to the contents of the interview, or to a part of the interview, for a specific time period. It is used when the information is highly confidential or controversial and should not be made public immediately.

Biographical Information Form: The oral history interviewee biography form contains basic biographical information about the narrator. It is filled out by the narrator, with help from the interviewer as necessary, before the interview.

Interview Information Form: The interview information form provides immediate archival control over the oral history interview. It contains information about the interviewer, narrator, the place and date of the interview, confirmation of the signing of the donor form, the number of cassettes used in the interview, and a brief abstract of the interview. It is filled out by the interviewer as soon as possible after the end of the interview.

Potential Narrator Information Form: Many projects use a form like this to keep track of possible narrators.

Master Log Form: Project coordinators use a form like this to maintain ongoing information on the status of the project.

Artifact and Archival Inventory Form: A form like this can help interviewers keep track of photographs, memorabilia, and other information the narrators may want to either give to the project or allow the narrator to take for copying. It should be filled out by the interviewer and should contain a complete list of all materials the narrator offers the interviewer. The interviewer should turn all items over to project coordinators as soon as possible after the interview. Project coordinators should then contact the narrator to determine disposition of the materials.

Oral History Donor Form

I, _____ (name of narrator), hereby give

to the _____ (designated repository) as a

donation this interview recorded on _____ (date). With this gift, I hereby

transfer to the _____ (designated repository) legal title

and all literary property rights to the interview, including copyright.

I understand the interview may be made available for research and such public programming as the

_____ (designated repository) may determine. This may

include use of the interview material in live or recorded programs for radio, television, cable, or any other

forms of electronic publishing that is not for profit. The interviews may not be broadcast, cablecast, or

electronically published for commercial purposes without my written consent.

Narrator's signature _____

Address _____

City, State, Zip Code _____

Date _____

Interviewer's signature _____

Address _____

City, State, Zip Code _____

Date _____

Oral History Donor Form (Restricted)

I, _____ (name of narrator), hereby give

to the _____ (designated repository) as a

donation this interview recorded on _____ (date). With this gift, I hereby

transfer to the _____ (designated repository) legal title

and all literary property rights to the interview, including copyright, with the exception that the

_____ (designated repository) shall allow access to the

interview until _____ (date) only to those persons having the written permis-

sion of _____ (name), his or her heirs, and his or her

designee(s) as specified below.

I understand the interviews may, after this time, be made available for research and such public pro-

gramming as the _____ (designated repository) may de-

termine. This may include use of the interview material in live or recorded programs for radio, television,

cable, or any other forms of electronic publishing that is not for profit. The interviews may not be broad-

cast, cablecast, or electronically published for commercial purposes without my written consent.

Narrator's signature _____

Address _____

City, State, Zip Code _____

Date _____

Specified heir(s) or designee(s): _____
(Please see interview master file for complete information)

Interviewer's signature _____

Address _____

City, State, Zip Code _____

Date _____

Interview Date _____

Biographical Information Form

Name _____

Address (home) _____

_____

Address (work) _____

_____

Telephone (home) _____ Telephone (work) _____ E-mail _____

Birth Date and Year _____

Birth Place _____

Profession _____

Spouse or Closest Living Relative _____

Maiden Name (if applicable) _____

Biographical Information (please include the names of parents, siblings, spouse, and children if applicable to the oral history interview):

Form Filled Out By _____

Date _____

Interview Information Form

Narrator's Name _____

Address _____

_____

Interviewer _____

Address _____

Interviewer Background Information _____

Date of Interview _____

Place of Interview _____

Length of Interview _____

Number of Cassettes or Discs _____

Oral History Donor Form Signed _____ (Date) _____

Unrestricted _____

Restricted _____

Transcript Reviewed by Narrator _____ (Date) _____

Abstract of Interview:

Potential Narrator Information Form

Name _____

Address _____

_____

Telephone (home) _____ Telephone (work) _____

E-mail _____ Fax _____

Potential Narrator File Information:

Form Filled Out By _____

Date _____

Master Log Form

Narrator	Interviewer	Interview Date	Release Signed (note type)	Draft Transcript to Narrator	Processing Done (note type and by whom)	Artifacts/Photos (cross reference to form)	Put In Repository

Artifact and Archival Inventory Form

Name _____

Address _____

_____

Item	Description	Status

Form Filled Out By _____

Date _____

Initial Contact Letter

Date _____

Dear _____ :

    I am contacting you on behalf of the _____ oral history project. Through this project, we are collecting information about_____ .

    As project coordinator, I am inviting you to be a part of this project. Your knowledge and insight will provide information about_____ .

    One of our project interviewers will call you within two weeks to discuss the project further and to answer any questions you may have. Your participation will involve a time commitment of two-three hours at a time and place convenient to you.

    I have enclosed a project brochure with this letter. I hope you will be able to participate in our project.

Sincerely yours,

Project Coordinator

_____ Oral History Project

Interview Confirmation Letter

Date _____

Dear _____ :

This letter confirms your oral history interview for the _____ oral

history project. It is scheduled at _____ on _____.
                                                    (time and place)   (date)

During the interview, we will cover the following topics:

List the topics you want to cover, such as:
—your background
—your first memories of the topic
—memories of (list specific items)
—your final thoughts

After the interview, I will ask you to sign a donor form giving it to _____ (repository).
The interview will be fully transcribed and, after you have reviewed the transcript, both tape and transcript will be turned over to them.

Thank you for agreeing to be part of this project. I look forward to meeting you. I can be reached at
_____ (telephone number) with any questions you may have.

Sincerely yours,

Interviewer

_____ Oral History Project

Thank You Letter

Date _____

Dear _____ :

Thank you for participating in an oral history interview for the _____
oral history project on _____ (date). The information you gave in your interview was very helpful. Your interview will be kept as part of the permanent collection of the
_____ (repository).

A review copy of the transcript for your interview will be completed and sent to you within a month.
When looking it over, please make sure all proper names are spelled correctly and that the transcriber has
accurately typed what you said. After you have returned your corrected transcript, we will make the
necessary changes and send you a final copy to thank you for participating in this project.

Thank you again for your time and your information.

Sincerely yours,

Interviewer

_____ Oral History Project

Sample Mission Statement

_____Oral History Project

The purpose of the _____ oral history project

is to document _____ through the personal

accounts of the men and women who were involved in or directly affected by those activities or events.

Designed to encompass the _____ as a study area, the project's

period of significance is _____. Through this project,

information about _____ not available or

documented elsewhere will be gathered and preserved at the _____ (name

of repository). All work will be performed according to the standards of the Oral History Association.

Sample Interview Outline

Jane Doe
February 18, 1998, 1:30 P.M.
249 Smith Place
Des Moines, Iowa

1. Describe self and family before going to the orphanage
    Reason for being placed in orphanage

2. First contact with orphanage
    Trip to orphanage
    First look at orphanage
    How handled when first arrived
    First contacts with other kids
    First contacts with matrons
    First contacts with other adults there
    Your thoughts at this time

3. Daily life at the orphanage during the first years you were there
    Describe cottage where you lived, located next to administrative building
    Describe matron in charge—M. Peterson
        Your relationship with her
        Her relationship with other children in the cottage
        Emotional support
        Cruelties
    Describe orphanage director, A. Swanson, and other administrators
        Their contact with children

    Describe other children in cottage and your relationship with them

    Daily routine—weekdays
    Daily routine—weekends
    Work expectations of you and other children
        Punishments—what, why, how, when, who
        Meals—describe
        Fun, play, recreation—describe
        Clothing

4. Routine different for boys and girls
    How and why
    Contact allowed between boys and girls
        Specific policies for siblings
            Affect on you and your brother

5. School life in the orphanage
    Describe schoolhouse and classrooms
    Describe teachers—P. Johnson, A. Anderson, D. Swenson
    Daily routine
        Subjects taught and how taught
            Reading, spelling, math, science
        Scholarly expectations for children
        Work expectations
        Punishments
        Fun, play, recreation

6. Holidays
    How celebrated
    Contact with family members
    Meals
    Gifts and institution's special ceremony in the 1940s when you lived there
    Religions, church attendance

7. Illnesses
    Describe hospital at orphanage and hospital director, Dr. Jones
    Describe medical care as you remember it
    Describe dental care
    Describe eye care, glasses and the like
    How handle epidemics
    How handle illnesses needing surgeries
    How handle chronic illnesses
    How handle emotional illnesses
    How handle deaths among orphans

8. Leaving orphanage
    When left and why
    Children who were adopted
    Children who were not adopted

9. Institutionalization
    Describe the effect of the orphanage experience on your life as you understand it
        Psychological
        Physical
        What it took from you
        What it gave to you

10. Legacy of the orphanage and its impact on you
    Overall impact on children there as you see and understand it

Processing Samples
Audio Interview with John Doe

Interviewed on October 16, 1989

Interviewed by Jane Smith

Interviewed for the
_____ Oral History Project

John Doe—JD
Jane Smith—JS

<u>Time Log</u>   Tape One, Side One

0.01   JS: This is Jane Smith with the _____ oral history project. I am here today on October 16, 1989, in Omaha, Nebraska, to talk with Mr. John Doe about his World War II experiences. I will start by asking you where you lived and what you were doing before World War II started.

JD: I was born in Lincoln, Nebraska. I graduated from Northeast High in the class of '42. I worked after high school until I got my "you're wanted" letter.

JS: Where were you when the attack on Pearl Harbor occurred [Dec. 7, 1941]?

0.03   JD: A bunch of us were in a filling station, all standing around a pot-bellied stove. There wasn't much to do on Sundays. It was a cold day. Somebody walked in the main door and asked, "Say gang, did you hear the latest?" We said, "What?" He said, "Pearl Harbor just got bombed!" Those were his words. We just kind of looked at him. "Pearl Harbor got bombed? Nobody can do that. That is an American naval base—isn't it? Nobody can get away with that."

With that, things began to build up and build up. It really took a full day before the American people were really aroused as to what had happened. As a matter of fact, [President Franklin D.] Roosevelt spoke at eleven o'clock the next morning. We had a convocation at Northeast High School. The entire student body went to the auditorium. They had several radios all over the auditorium and, as Roosevelt spoke, everybody applauded.

0.05   There was no school that day. We walked up and down the halls. We were making big patriotic signs on the blackboards—shaking hands with the British. Everybody was drawing on the blackboards. "We'll show them!" There was a great deal of nationalism that just came overnight.

Tape Log

Oral History Interview with James Doe

Interviewed on July 12, 1993

Interviewed by John Smith

Interviewed for the
_____ Oral History Project

<u>Time Count in Minutes</u>   <u>Description of Interview Content</u>

Tape One, Side One

0.0   Beginning of interview.

5.0   Personal background, description of economic difficulties, narrator's education, difficulties for rest of family.

10.0   Entry into the Civilian Conservation Corps. Hearing about opportunity to enroll in CCC, where to enroll, how to enroll.

15.0   Leaving home for CCC camp. First time away from home. Learning about which camp assigned to. Other black enrollees.

20.0   Description of CCC camp. Where located, number of buildings, what buildings built of, how arranged.

25.0   Description of barracks and mess hall. Specific descriptions of where Doe slept and ate. Separation from white enrollees.

30.0   Clothing issues. Description of summer and winter issues of clothing. World War I surplus items.

Tape One, Side Two

0.0   Camps run by U.S. Army. "We called the army our mother, because it fed and clothed us." Forest service was work agency. Work assignments for black enrollees.

Video Interview with Jane Doe

Interviewed by John Smith

Interviewed on March 19, 1997

Interviewed for the
_____ Oral History Project

Jane Doe—JD
John Smith—JS

Tape One, Side One

01:01:10 Q: I am speaking with Mrs. Jane Doe about her childhood and memories of her family. This interview, made at her home on March 19, 1997, is a follow-up to an audio interview with Mrs. Doe. During our earlier interview, you spoke about your background in riding and showing horses. How did that get started?

01:08:15 A: We had such fun with our horses when I was a child. We used to teach the ponies little tricks. And then we always had to have a big show. It was held at Mainhall. We would gather all the children to ride, you see.

01:12:20 A: We taught little King to lie down. And he would tell you how old he was or how old you were by shaking his foot or shaking his head. And then he would lie down—tell him to lie down and go to sleep.

01:16:50 A: Well, then, one time we got pulled away from where the horses were after we had done that. And King lay there on the ground with his eyes closed tight. I bet he was there for half an hour. He could stand on a barrel, too. That was the other trick he could do.

Bust
Retake

01:17:12 Q: Let's talk about your memories of holidays with your children.

01:17:20 A: We used to go East for Christmas. I thought, well, let's try it and see. They've never been on a train. Let's try it. And in those days, trains were [inaudible].

**INTERVIEW WITH
JANE DOE**

_____ **ORAL HISTORY PROJECT**

Interviewed by John Smith
July 23, 2001

 *Oral History Evaluation Guidelines*

**Oral History Association
Pamphlet Number 3
Adopted 1989, Revised Sept. 2000**

Table of Contents

Foreword

Since its founding in 1967 the Oral History Association (OHA) has grappled constantly with developing and promoting professional standards for oral historians. This has been no easy task, given the creative, dynamic, and multidisciplinary nature of the field. The OHA has sought to encourage the creation of recorded interviews that are as complete, verifiable, and usable as possible, and to discourage both inadequate interviewing and the misuse of history. Yet it recognizes that oral historians cannot afford to suppress ingenuity and inspiration nor to ignore new developments in scholarship and technology.

The OHA issued its first "goals and guidelines" in 1968, broadly stating the principles, rights, and obligations that all interviewees, interviewers, and sponsoring institutions needed to take into consideration. Then in 1979, at the prompting of various granting agencies, leaders of the OHA met at the Wingspread Conference Center in Racine, Wisconsin, to produce a set of "evaluation guidelines." These guidelines have since provided invaluable assistance to oral history projects of all sizes and purposes. Organized in checklist form, they offered reminders of the myriad of issues involved in conducting, processing, and preserving oral history interviews. Not every guideline applied to every project, but taken together they provided a common ground for dialogue among oral historians.

Over the next decade, new issues arose. When the need for revision of the earlier guidelines became apparent, the OHA decided against convening another special meeting, as done at Wingspread, and instead appointed four committees to examine those sections of the evaluation guidelines that required revision or entirely new material. After a year's work, the committees presented their proposals to the members of the Association at the annual meeting, Galveston, Texas, in 1989, where their reports were discussed, amended, and adopted at the general business meeting. During the next year, the chairs of the four evaluation guidelines committees analyzed, revised, and expanded the Goals and Guidelines into a new Statement of Principles and Standards. They offered these standards for amendment and adoption by the membership at the annual meeting in Cambridge, Massachusetts, in November 1990.

If that process sounds convoluted, it was. But its many stages were designed deliberately to foster thoughtful debate among the widest cross-section of oral history practitioners. As a result, the new standards and guidelines more specifically addressed the needs of independent and unaffiliated researchers, as well as those of the larger oral history programs and archives. They dealt with the problems and potentials of videotaped interviews. They raised issues about the use of oral history in the classroom by teachers and students.

The most intense discussions predictably dealt with ethical issues. A greater awareness of the effects of race, class, gender, ethnicity, and culture on interviewing, together with a heightened concern over the impact that the oral history projects might have on the communities in which the interviews were conducted, were woven into both the Evaluation Guidelines and the Statement of Principles and Standards. The new guidelines and standards encouraged oral historians to make their interviews accessible to the community and to consider sharing the rewards and recognition that might result from their projects with their interviewees. They also sanctioned the use of anonymous interviews, although only in "extremely sensitive" circumstances.

During the 1990s, the rapid advances in technology required yet another revision on the new ways of recording, preserving, using and distributing oral history. In 1998 an ad hoc committee presented additional revisions for discussion and adoption by the membership at the annual meeting in Buffalo, New York. These revisions included new sections on recording equipment and tape preservation, and aimed to encourage practitioners to pay more attention to technical standards and to new technology and media, particularly the Internet. At the same time they raised some of the ethical issues that the new technology posed.

All of those who labored in the preparation of the principles and standards and the evaluation guidelines trust that they will offer positive assistance to anyone conducting oral history interviews. While these guidelines and standards provide a basis for peer judgment and review, their success will ultimately depend more on the willingness of the individual oral historians and oral history projects to apply them to their own work.

Donald A. Ritchie

Evaluation Guidelines Committees
1988–1989
Donald A. Ritchie (coordinator), U.S. Senate Historical Office

Committee on Ethical/Legal Guidelines
Sherna B. Gluck (co-chair), California State University Long Beach
Linda Shopes (co-chair), Pennsylvania Historical & Museum Commission
Albert S. Broussard, Texas A&M University
John A. Neuenschwander, Carthage College

Committee on Independent/Unaffiliated Research
Terry L. Birdwhistell (chair), University of Kentucky
Jo Blatti, Old Independence Regional Museum
Maurice Maryanow
Holly C. Shulman, Washington, D.C.

Committee on the Use of Videotape
Pamela M. Henson (chair), Smithsonian Institution
David H. Mould, Ohio University
James B. Murray, Shomberg Library
Terri A. Schorzman, Smithsonian Institution
Margaret Robertson, Minnesota Historical Society

Education Committee
George L. Mehaffy (chair)
Patricia Grimmer
Denise Joseph
Rebecca Sharpless, Baylor University
Andor Skotnes, Sage Colleges
Richard Williams, Plum Borough Senior High School

Principles and Standards Committee, 1989–1990
Donald A. Ritchie (chair), U.S. Senate Historical Office
Willa K. Baum, University of California Berkeley
Terry L. Birdwhistell, University of Kentucky
Sherna B. Gluck, California State University Long Beach
Pamela M. Henson, Smithsonian Institution
Linda Shopes, Pennsylvania Historical & Museum Commission
Ronald E. Marcello (ex officio), University of North Texas
Lila J. Goff (ex officio), Minnesota Historical Society

Technology Update Committee, 1998
Sherna Gluck (chair), California State University Long Beach
Charles Hardy, Westchester University
Marjorie McLellan, Miami University
Roy Rosenzweig, George Mason University

Principles and Standards of the Oral History Association

The Oral History Association promotes oral history as a method of gathering and preserving historical information through recorded interviews with participants in past events and ways of life. It encourages those who produce and use oral history to recognize certain principles, rights, technical standards, and obligations for the creation and preservation of source material that is authentic, useful, and reliable. These include obligations to the interviewee, to the profession, and to the public, as well as mutual obligations between sponsoring organizations and interviewers.

People with a range of affiliations and sponsors conduct oral history interviews for a variety of purposes: to create archival records, for individual research, for community and institutional projects, and for publications and media productions. While these principles and standards provide a general framework for guiding professional conduct, their application may vary according to the nature of specific oral history projects. Regardless of the purpose of the interviews, oral history should be conducted in the spirit of critical inquiry and social responsibility and with a recognition of the interactive and subjective nature of the enterprise.

Responsibility to Interviewees:
1. Interviewees should be informed of the purposes and procedures of oral history in general and of the aims and anticipated uses of the particular projects to which they are making their contributions.

2. Interviewees should be informed of the mutual rights in the oral history process, such as editing, access restrictions, copyrights, prior use, royalties, and the expected disposition and dissemination of all forms of the record, including the potential for electronic distribution.
3. Interviewees should be informed that they will be asked to sign a legal release. Interviews should remain confidential until interviewees have given permission for their use.
4. Interviewers should guard against making promises to interviewees that the interviewers may not be able to fulfill, such as guarantees of publication and control over the use of interviews after they have been made public. In all future uses, however, good faith efforts should be made to honor the spirit of the interviewee's agreement.
5. Interviews should be conducted in accord with any prior agreements made with the interviewee, and such agreements should be documented for the record.
6. Interviewers should work to achieve a balance between the objectives of the project and the perspectives of the interviewees. They should be sensitive to the diversity of social and cultural experiences and to the implications of race, gender, class, ethnicity, age, religion, and sexual orientation. They should encourage interviewees to respond in their own style and language and to address issues that reflect their concerns. Interviewers should fully explore all appropriate areas of inquiry with the interviewee and not be satisfied with superficial responses.
7. Interviewers should guard against possible exploitation of interviewees and be sensitive to the ways in which their interviews might be used. Interviewers must respect the rights of interviewees to refuse to discuss certain subjects, to restrict access to the interview, or, under Guidelines extreme circumstances, even to choose anonymity. Interviewers should clearly explain these options to all interviewees.
8. Interviewers should use the best recording equipment within their means to accurately reproduce the interviewee's voice and, if appropriate, other sounds as well as visual images.
9. Given the rapid development of new technologies, interviewees should be informed of the wide range of potential uses of their interviews.
10. Good faith efforts should be made to ensure that the uses of recordings and transcripts comply with both the letter and spirit of the interviewee's agreement.

Responsibility to the Public and to the Profession:
1. Oral historians have a responsibility to maintain the highest professional standards in the conduct of their work and to uphold the standards of the various disciplines and professions with which they are affiliated.
2. In recognition of the importance of oral history to an understanding of the past and of the cost and effort involved, interviewers and interviewees should mutually strive to record candid information of lasting value and to make that information accessible.
3. Interviewees should be selected based on the relevance of their experiences to the subject at hand.
4. Interviewers should possess interviewing skills as well as professional competence and knowledge of the subject at hand.
5. Regardless of the specific interests of the project, interviewers should attempt to extend the inquiry beyond the specific focus of the project to create as complete a record as possible for the benefit of others.
6. Interviewers should strive to prompt informative dialogue through challenging and perceptive inquiry. They should be grounded in the background of the persons being interviewed and, when possible, should carefully research appropriate documents and secondary sources related to subjects about which the interviewees can speak.
7. Interviewers should make every effort to record their interviews using the best recording equipment within their means to reproduce accurately the interviewee's voice and, if appropriate, image. They also should collect and record other historical documentation the interviewee may possess, including still photographs, print materials, and other sound and moving image recordings, if appropriate.
8. Interviewers should provide complete documentation of their preparation and methods, including the circumstances of the interviews.
9. Interviewers and, when possible, interviewees should review and evaluate their interviews, including any summaries or transcriptions made from them.

10. With the permission of the interviewees, interviewers should arrange to deposit their interviews in an archival repository that is capable of both preserving the interviews and eventually making them available for general use. Interviewers should provide basic information about the interviews, including project goals, sponsorship, and funding. Preferably, interviewers should work with repositories before conducting the interviews to determine necessary legal Guidelines arrangements. If interviewers arrange to retain first use of the interviews, it should be only for a reasonable time before public use.

11. Interviewers should be sensitive to the communities from which they have collected oral histories, taking care not to reinforce thoughtless stereotypes nor to bring undue notoriety to them. Interviewers should take every effort to make the interviews accessible to the communities.

12. Oral history interviews should be used and cited with the same care and standards applied to other historical sources. Users have a responsibility to retain the integrity of the interviewee's voice, neither misrepresenting the interviewee's words nor taking them out of context.

13. Sources of funding or sponsorship of oral history projects should be made public in all exhibits, media presentations, or publications that result from the projects.

14. Interviewers and oral history programs should conscientiously consider how they might share with interviewees and their communities the rewards and recognition that might result from their work.

Responsibility for Sponsoring and Archival Institutions:

1. Institutions sponsoring and maintaining oral history archives have a responsibility to interviewees, interviewers, the profession, and the public to maintain the highest technical, professional, and ethical standards in the creation and archival preservation of oral history interviews and related materials.

2. Subject to conditions that interviewees set, sponsoring institutions (or individual collectors) have an obligation to: prepare and preserve easily usable records; keep abreast of rapidly developing technologies for preservation and dissemination; keep accurate records of the creation and processing of each interview; and identify, index, and catalog interviews.

3. Sponsoring institutions and archives should make known through a variety of means, including electronic modes of distribution, the existence of interviews open for research.

4. Within the parameters of their missions and resources, archival institutions should collect interviews generated by independent researchers and assist interviewers with the necessary legal agreements.

5. Sponsoring institutions should train interviewers. Such training should: provide them basic instruction in how to record high fidelity interviews and, if appropriate, other sound and moving image recordings; explain the objectives of the program to them; inform them of all ethical and legal considerations governing an interview; and make clear to interviewers what their obligations are to the program and to the interviewees.

6. Interviewers and interviewees should receive appropriate acknowledgment for their work in all forms of citation or usage.

7. Archives should make good faith efforts to ensure that uses of recordings and transcripts, especially those that employ new technologies, comply with both the letter and spirit of the interviewee's agreement.

Oral History Evaluation Guidelines
Program/Project Guidelines

Purposes and Objectives
a. Are the purposes clearly set forth? How realistic are they?
b. What factors demonstrate a significant need for the project?
c. What is the research design? How clear and realistic is it?

d. Are the terms, conditions, and objectives of funding clearly made known to judge the potential effect of such funding on the scholarly integrity of the project? Is the allocation of funds adequate to allow the project goals to be accomplished?

e. How do institutional relationships affect the purposes and objectives?

Selection of Recording Equipment

a. Should the interview be recorded on sound or visual recording equipment?

b. Are the best possible recording equipment and media available within one's budget being used?

c. Are interviews recorded on a medium that meets archival preservation standards?

d. How well has the interviewer mastered use of the equipment upon which the interview will be recorded?

Selection of Interviewers and Interviewees

a. In what ways are the interviewers and interviewees appropriate (or inappropriate) to the purposes and objectives?

b. What are the significant omissions and why were they omitted?

Records and Provenance

a. What are the policies and provisions for maintaining a record of the provenance of interviews? Are they adequate? What can be done to improve them?

b. How are records, policies, and procedures made known to interviewers, interviewees, staff, and users?

c. How does the system of records enhance the usefulness of the interviews and safeguard the rights of those involved?

Availability of Materials

a. How accurate and specific is the publicizing of the interviews?

b. How is information about interviews directed to likely users? Have new media and electronic methods of distribution been considered to publicize materials and make them available?

c. How have the interviews been used?

Finding Aids

a. What is the overall design for finding aids?

b. Are the finding aids adequate and appropriate?

c. How available are the finding aids?

d. Have new technologies been used to develop the most effective finding aids?

Management, Qualifications, and Training

a. How effective is the management of the program/project?

b. What are the provisions for supervision and staff review?

c. What are the qualifications for staff positions?

d. What are the provisions for systematic and effective training?

e. What improvements could be made in the management of the program/project?

Ethical/Legal Guidelines

What procedures are followed to assure that interviewers/programs recognize and honor their responsibility to the interviewees? Specifically, what procedures are used to assure that:

a. the interviewees are made fully aware of the goals and objectives of the oral history program/project?

b. the interviewees are made fully aware of the various stages of the program/project and the nature of their participation at each stage?

c. the interviewees are given the opportunity to respond to questions as freely as possible and are not subjected to stereotyped assumptions based on race, ethnicity, gender, class, or any other social/cultural characteristic?

d. the interviewees understand their rights to refuse to discuss certain subjects, to seal portions of the interviews, or in extremely sensitive circumstances even to choose to remain anonymous?

e. the interviewees are fully informed about the potential uses of the material, including deposit of the interviews in a repository, publication in all forms of print or electronic media, including the Internet or other emerging technologies, and all forms of public programming?

f. the interviewees are provided a full and easily comprehensible explanation of their legal rights before being asked to sign a contract or deed of gift transferring rights, title, and interest in the tape(s) and transcript(s) to an administering authority or individual?

g. care is taken so that the distribution and use of the material complies with the letter and spirit of the interviewees' agreements?

h. all prior agreements made with the interviewees are honored?

i. the interviewees are fully informed about the potential for and disposition of royalties that might accrue from the use of their interviews, including all forms of public programming?

j. the interviews and any other related materials will remain confidential until the interviewees have released their contents?

What procedures are followed to assure that interviewers/programs recognize and honor their responsibilities to the profession? Specifically, what procedures assure that:

a. the interviewer has considered the potential for public programming and research use of the interviews and has endeavored to prevent any exploitation of or harm to interviewees?

b. the interviewer is well trained to conduct the interview in a professional manner, including the use of appropriate recording equipment and media?

c. the interviewer is well grounded in the background of the subject(s) to be discussed?

d. the interview will be conducted in a spirit of critical inquiry and that efforts will be made to provide as complete a historical record as possible?

e. the interviewees are selected based on the relevance of their experience to the subject at hand and that an appropriate cross-section of interviewees is selected for any particular project?

f. the interview materials, including recordings, transcripts, relevant photographic, moving image, and sound documents as well as agreements and documentation of the interview process, will be placed in a repository after a reasonable period of time, subject to the agreements made with the interviewee and that the repository will administer their use in accordance with those agreements?

g. the methodologies of the program/project, as well as its goals and objectives, are available for the general public to evaluate?

h. the interview materials have been properly cataloged, including appropriate acknowledgment and credit to the interviewer, and that their availability for research use is made known?

What procedures are followed to assure that interviewers and programs are aware of their mutual responsibilities and obligations? Specifically, what procedures are followed to assure that:

a. interviewers are made aware of the program goals and are fully informed of ethical and legal considerations?

b. interviewers are fully informed of all the tasks they are expected to complete in an oral history project?

c. interviewers are made fully aware of their obligations to the oral history program/sponsoring institution, regardless of their own personal interest in a program/project?

d. programs/sponsoring institutions treat their interviewers equitably by providing for appropriate compensation, acknowledging all products resulting from their work, and supporting fieldwork practices consistent with professional standards whenever there is a conflict between the parties to the interview?

e. interviewers are fully informed of their legal rights and of their responsibilities to both the interviewee and to the sponsoring institution?

What procedures are followed to assure that interviewers and programs recognize and honor their responsibilities to the community/public? Specifically, what procedures assure that:

a. the oral history materials and all works created from them will be available and accessible to the community that participated in the project?
b. sources of extramural funding and sponsorship are clearly noted for each interview of project?
c. the interviewers and project endeavor not to impose their own values on the community being studied?
d. the tapes and transcripts will not be used unethically?

Recording Preservation Guidelines

Recognizing the significance of the recording for historical and cultural analysis and the potential uses of oral history interviews in nonprint media, what procedures are followed to assure that:

a. appropriate care and storage of the original recordings begins immediately after their creation?
b. the original recordings are duplicated and stored according to accepted archival standards [i.e. stored in closed boxes in a cool, dry, dust-free environment]?
c. original recordings are reduplicated onto the best preservation media before significant deterioration occurs?
d. every effort is made in duplicating tapes to preserve a faithful facsimile of the interviewee's voice?
e. all transcribing, auditing, and other uses are done from a duplicate, not the original recording?

Tape/Transcript Processing Guidelines

Information about the Participants
a. Are the names of both interviewer and interviewee clearly indicated on the tape/abstract/transcript and in catalog materials?
b. Is there adequate biographical information about both interviewer and interviewee? Where can it be found?

Interview Information
a. Are the tapes, transcripts, time indices, abstracts, and other materials presented for use identified as to the program/project of which they are a part?
b. Are the date and place of the interview indicated on the tape, transcript, time index, and abstract and in appropriate catalog material?
c. Are there interviewers' statements about the preparation for or circumstances of the interviews? Where? Are they generally available to researchers? How are the rights of the interviewees protected against improper use of such commentaries?
d. Are there records of contracts between the program and the interviewee? How detailed are they? Are they available to researchers? If so, with what safeguards for individual rights and privacy?

Interview Tape Information
a. Is the complete original tape preserved? Are there one or more duplicate copies?
b. If the original or any duplicate has been edited, rearranged, cut, or spliced in any way, is there a record of that action, including by whom, when, and for what purposes the action was taken?
c. Do the tape label and appropriate catalog materials show the recording speed, level, and length of the interview? If videotaped, do the tape label and appropriate catalog information show the format (e.g., U-Matic, VHS, 8mm, etc.) and scanning system and clearly indicate the tracks on which the audio and time code have been recorded?
d. In the absence of transcripts, are there suitable finding aids to give users access to information on the tapes? What form do they take? Is there a record of who prepared these finding aids?
e. Are researchers permitted to listen to or view the tapes? Are there any restrictions on the use of the tapes?

Interview Transcript Information

a. Is the transcript an accurate record of the tape? Is a careful record kept of each step of processing the transcript, including who transcribed, audited, edited, retyped, and proofread the transcripts in final copy?

b. Are the nature and extent of changes in the transcript from the original tape made known to the user?

c. What finding aids have been prepared for the transcript? Are they suitable and adequate? How could they be improved?

d. Are there any restrictions on access to or use of the transcripts? Are they clearly noted?

e. Are there any photo materials or other supporting documents for the interview? Do they enhance and supplement the text?

f. If videotaped, does the transcript contain time references and annotation describing the complementary visuals on the videotape?

Interview Content Guidelines

Does the content of each interview and the cumulative content of the whole collection contribute to accomplishing the objectives of the program/project?

a. In what particulars does each interview or the whole collection succeed or fall short of the objectives of the project or program?

b. Do audio and visual tapes in the collection avoid redundancy and supplement one another in interview content and focus?

In what ways does the program/project contribute to historical understanding?

a. In what particulars does each interview or the whole collection succeed or fall short in making such a contribution?

b. To what extent does the material add fresh information, fill gaps in the existing record, and/or provide fresh insights and perspectives?

c. To what extent is the information reliable and valid? Is it eyewitness or hearsay evidence? How well and in what manner does it meet internal and external tests of corroboration, consistency, and explication of contradictions?

d. What is the relationship of the interview information to existing documentation and historiography?

e. How does the texture of the interview impart detail, richness, and flavor to the historical record?

f. What is the nature of the information contributed? Is it facts, perceptions, interpretations, judgments, or attitudes, and how does each contribute to understanding?

g. Are the scope, volume, and representativeness of the population interviewed appropriate and sufficient to the purpose? Is there enough testimony to validate the evidence without passing the point of diminishing returns? How appropriate is the quantity to the purposes of the study?

h. How do the form and structure of the interviews contribute to making the content understandable?

i. To what extent does the audio and/or video recording capture unique sound and visual information?

j. Do the visual and other sound elements complement and/or supplement the verbal information? Has the interview captured processes, objects, or other individuals in the visual and sound environment?

Interview Conduct Guidelines

Use of Other Sources

a. Is the oral history technique the best way to acquire the information? If not, what other sources exist? Has the interviewer used them and sought to preserve them if necessary?

b. Has the interviewer made an effort to consult other relevant oral histories?

c. Is the interview technique a valuable way to supplement existing sources?

d. Do videotaped interviews complement, not duplicate, existing still or moving visual images?

Interviewer Preparation

a. Is the interviewer well informed about the subjects under discussion?
b. Are the primary and secondary sources used to prepare for the interview adequate?
c. Has the interviewer mastered the use of appropriate recording equipment and the field- recording techniques that insure a high-fidelity recording?

Interviewee Selection and Orientation

a. Does the interviewee seem appropriate to the subjects discussed?
b. Does the interviewee understand and respond to the interview purposes?
c. Has the interviewee prepared for the interview and assisted in the process?
d. If a group interview, have composition and group dynamics been considered in selecting participants?

Interviewer-Interviewee Relations

a. Do interviewer and interviewee collaborate with each other toward interview objectives?
b. Is there a balance between empathy and analytical judgment in the interview?
c. If videotaped, is the interviewer/interviewee relationship maintained despite the presence of a technical crew? Do the technical personnel understand how a videotaped oral history interview differs from a scripted production?

Technique and Adaptive Skills

a. In what ways does the interview show that the interviewer has used skills appropriate to: the interviewee's condition (health, memory, mental alertness, ability to communicate, time schedule, etc.) and the interview location and conditions (disruptions and interruptions, equipment problems, extraneous participants, background noises, etc.)?
b. What evidence is there that the interviewer has: thoroughly explored pertinent lines of thought? followed up on significant clues? made an effort to identify sources of information? employed critical challenges when needed? thoroughly explored the potential of the visual environment, if videotaped?
c. Has the progam/project used recording equipment and media that are appropriate for the purposes of the work and potential nonprint as well as print uses of the material? Are the recordings of the highest appropriate technical quality? How could they be improved?
d. If videotaped, are lighting, composition, camera work, and sound of the highest appropriate technical quality?
e. In the balance between content and technical quality, is the technical quality good without subordinating the interview process?

Perspective

a. Do the biases of the interviewer interfere with or influence the responses of the interviewee?
b. What information is available that may inform the users of any prior or separate relationship between the interviewer and interviewee?

Historical Contribution

a. Does the interviewer pursue the inquiry with historical integrity?
b. Do other purposes being served by the interview enrich or diminish quality?
c. What does the interview contribute to the larger context of historical knowledge and understanding?

Independent/Unaffiliated Researcher Guidelines

Creation and Use of Interviews

a. Has the independent/unaffiliated researcher followed the guidelines for obtaining interviews as suggested in the Program/Project Guideline section?
b. Have proper citation and documentation been provided in works created (books, articles, audio-visual

productions, or other public presentations) to inform users of the work about the interviews used and the permanent location of the interviews?

c. Do works created include an explanation of the interview project, including editorial procedures?

d. Has the independent/unaffiliated researcher arranged to deposit the works created in an appropriate repository?

Transfer of Interviews to Archival Repository

a. Has the independent/unaffiliated researcher properly obtained the agreement of the repository before making representations about the disposition of the interviews?

b. Is the transfer consistent with agreements or understandings with interviewees? Were legal agreements obtained from interviewees?

c. Has the researcher provided the repository with adequate descriptions of the creation of the interviews and the project?

d. What is the technical quality of the recorded interviews? Are the interviews transcribed, abstracted, or indexed, and, if so, what is the quality?

Educator and Student Guidelines

Has the educator:

a. become familiar with the "Oral History Evaluation Guidelines" and conveyed their substance to the student?

b. ensured that each student is properly prepared before going into the community to conduct oral history interviews, including familiarization with the ethical issues surrounding oral history and the obligation to seek the informed consent of the interviewee?

c. become familiar with the literature, recording equipment, techniques, and processes of oral history so that the best possible instruction can be presented to the student?

d. worked with other professionals and organizations to provide the best oral history experience for the student?

e. considered that the project may merit preservation and worked with other professionals and repositories to preserve and disseminate these collected materials?

f. shown willingness to share expertise with other educators, associations, and organizations?

Has the student:

a. become thoroughly familiar with the equipment, techniques, and processes of oral history interviewing and the development of research using oral history interviews?

b. explained to the interviewee the purpose of the interview and how it will be used and obtained the interviewee's informed consent to participate?

c. treated the interviewee with respect?

d. signed a receipt for and returned any materials borrowed from the interviewee?

e. obtained a signed legal release for the interview?

f. kept her/his word about oral or written promises made to the interviewee?

g. given proper credit (oral or written) when using oral testimony and used the material in context?

From the Oral History Association, "Pamphlet Number 3" (Carlisle, Pa.: Oral History Association, adopted 1989, revised September 2000). Copyright © 2000 by the Oral History Association. Reprinted with permission.

Abstract: A one- or two-page summary of the interview contents.

Acid-free: There are no consistent standards for acid-free paper and many consumer products, while labeled acid-free on the shelf, will develop damaging acids as time goes on. Generally, this term means paper that is lignin-free and alkaline with a pH greater than 7. Lignin is an acidic element found in wood products. Alkaline is the opposite of acidic.

Analog: A recording process that prints sound in a continuous pattern on magnetic tape, either in cassette or reel-to-reel format.

Audit-check: An interview processing step, this refers to carefully listening to the interview while reading the transcript, catching any transcription errors.

Biography Information Form: A part of the interview record-keeping system, this form contains background information about the narrator.

Broadcast quality: Specifications defined by the National Television Standards Committee and the Advanced Television Systems Committee of the Federal Communications Commission for the level of quality at which radio or television stations will transmit.

Copyright: The exclusive legal right to print or otherwise reproduce, publish, or sell copies of original materials (such as oral history interviews) and to license their production and sale by others.

Digital: A recording process that stores sound as bits of data, the way a computer stores information, using either digital audiotape or compact discs.

Donor Form: Transfers copyright of an oral history interview to the designated owner/repository. Signed by both the narrator and the interviewer, and any other person whose voice is heard on the tape or disc, as soon as the interview session ends even if more interviews are planned with the narrator.

Interview Information Form: The first step in processing the interview, it identifies the narrator and interviewer, documents the date of the interview and its length, and contains a short abstract or summary of the interview contents.

Interviewer: The person responsible for conducting the oral history interview. Should have both general and interview-specific information, understand and be able to use open-ended questioning techniques, be able to build effective human relationships in the interview setting, and work according to the standards of the Oral History Association.

Life interview: A series of oral history interviews with one person, usually resulting in an autobiographical set of materials.

Master file: Contains all information about an interview; is permanently kept with the interview master.

Narrator (interviewee): A person with first-hand knowledge about the subject or topic of the interview and with the capability to effectively communicate this information.

Oral history: Primary resource material created in a recorded interview setting with a witness to or a participant in an historical event for the purpose of collecting and preserving the person's first-hand information and making it available to researchers.

Oral History Association: The national professional organization for practitioners of oral history. It supports and encourages an understanding of the ethical principles and standards that guide oral historians in their work.

Oral history interview: The recorded question-and-answer session between an interviewer and narrator characterized by well-focused, clearly stated, open-ended, neutral questions aimed at gathering information not available from other sources. Usually lasts about one-and-one-half hours.

Oral history project: A series of individual oral history interviews recorded one at a time with a number of narrators focusing on one subject, topic, or event.

Potential Narrator Information Form: The record-keeping form that contains information about potential project narrators. One form is kept for each name.

Preservation master: The original interview recording. It should be kept intact to preserve the full interview. Kept in permanent and appropriate storage with the master files; user copies are made from these for interview access and processing.

Primary resource: Provides first-hand information with no interpretation between the document and the researcher. Examples are a diary, correspondence such as letters from family members, a family Bible, or government records.

Processing: The steps taken to make interview information accessible to present and future users.

Repository: The place where oral history project information is deposited and permanently kept.

Tape log: An annotated list of information covered in the interview. Done at timed intervals, it notes each new subject and the information discussed at the specific intervals.

Transcript: A verbatim, printed copy of the interview. It matches the interview as closely as possible and contains the full and accurately spelled names of all persons and places mentioned in the interview. Transcripts are often subject-indexed.

Many books deal with various aspects of oral history and its interpretation and uses. This bibliography contains examples of some standard works and some of the more recent writing in the field.

Oral History

Allen, Barbara, and Lynwood Montell. *From Memory to History: Using Oral Sources in Local Historical Research.* Jackson: University Press of Mississippi, 1991. Allen and Montell discuss uses of oral information as a way of documenting local history. The term "oral sources" in the title reflects their backgrounds as folklorists.

Baum, Willa. *Oral History for the Local Historical Society.* Nashville: American Association for State and Local History, 1987. And Baum, Willa. *Transcribing and Editing Oral History.* Nashville: American Association for State and Local History, 1977. Oral historians owe a debt to Willa Baum's ground-breaking work in these two volumes.

Bunch, Lonnie G., editor. *Pathways: Discovering Your Connections to History.* Nashville: American Association for State and Local History, 2002. This booklet presents an interdisciplinary approach to exploring family and community history that draws on solid research and the best practices of oral historians, folklorists, and local historians.

Dean, Pamela, Toby Daspit, and Petra Munro. *Talking Gumbo: A Teacher's Guide to Using Oral History in the Classroom.* Baton Rouge: T. Harry Williams Center for Oral History, 1998. This book, written as a companion guide to the video *You've Got to Hear This Story*, was developed specifically for classroom use of oral history. As its title states, it is a teacher's guide and, as such, it includes sections on why and how oral history can be added to the curriculum, how it strengthens other skills, suggested lesson plans, and an extensive bibliography of secondary school oral history materials. The video, designed for use in grades eight through twelve, uses student actors to play various roles in teaching interviewing specifics.

Dunaway, David K., and Willa Baum, editors. *Oral History: An Interdisciplinary Anthology*, 2d ed. Walnut Creek, Calif.: AltaMira Press, 1996. This collection of essays from leading oral historians was written for people who already have a background in oral history and are interested in learning more. Divided into five parts—"The Gateway to Oral History," "Interpreting and Designing Oral History," "Oral History Applied: Local, Ethnic, Family, and Women's History," "Oral History and Related Disciplines: Folklore, Anthropology, Media, and Librarianship," and "Oral History and Regional Studies"—it contains materials by Allan Nevins, Louis Starr, Ronald J. Grele, William Moss, Amelia Fry, Linda Shopes, Paul Thompson, Alessandro Portelli, Sherna Gluck, the editors of the book, and many others.

Frisch, Michael H. *A Shared Authority: Essays on the Craft and Meaning of Oral and Public History.* Albany: State University of New York Press, 1990. In this book, Frisch discusses how oral history and public history help people develop a sense of the past.

Edward D. Ives. *The Tape-Recorded Interview: A Manual for Fieldworkers in Folklore and Oral History*, 2d ed. Knoxville: University of Tennessee Press, 1995. In this book, Ives describes a careful, methodological approach to the interview process. He also discusses recording music, doing group interviews, and using props, such as photographs, during the interview.

Journal of American History. Published quarterly by the Organization of American Historians, it has included a section on oral history in the September issue since 1987. Information in this section generally focuses on the uses and interpretations of oral history in the study of specific historical topics.

Linde, Charlotte. *Life Stories: The Creation of Coherence.* Oxford: Oxford University Press, 1993. Linde's work provokes thought about the subtleties and layers of meaning communicated in life history interviews.

Matters, Marion. *Oral History Cataloging Manual.* Chicago: Society of American Archivists, 1995. The standard oral history cataloging manual.

Portelli, Alessandro. *The Death of Luigi Trastulli and Other Stories: Form and Meaning in Oral History.* Albany: State University of New York Press, 1991. Portelli is one of the leaders in discussions about the meaning and subjectivity of oral history. In this book, using examples from oral histories about the death of an Italian worker shortly after World War II and other interviews, he discusses issues of reliability and validity of memory, putting them into the context of people's interpretations of their lives.

Ritchie, Donald A. *Doing Oral History.* New York: Twayne Publishers, 1995. Using a question-and-answer format appropriate for a thorough discussion of oral history, this book covers such topics as starting a project, the uses of oral history, preservation issues, and teaching oral history. By focusing in detail on all phases of oral history, this book helps practitioners gain an understanding of the complexities of the field. The extensive bibliography is an excellent source of additional information on work in the field.

Suquamish Oral History Project. *A Guide for Oral History in the Native American Community,* 3d ed. Suquamish: Suquamish Tribal Cultural Center, 2000. This publication provides information and insight about oral history in the Native American community.

Thompson, Paul. *The Voice of the Past,* 3d ed. Oxford: Oxford University Press, 2000. In this book, Thompson provides an analytical look at many topics important to oral historians, including a comparative look at the place of oral history in the community, the achievements of oral history, its use as evidence, the relationship between memory and self, and interpreting the interview results. It was written both as a practical guide about collecting and using oral history and to provoke historians to ask themselves what they are doing and why.

Vaz, Kim Marie, editor. *Oral Narrative Research with Black Women.* Thousand Oaks, Calif.: Sage Publications, 1997. This is a collection of essays about oral history work with black women. Essayists include Martia Graham Goodson, Joycelyn Moody, Christine Obbo, Arlene Hambrick, Georgia W. Brown, Renee' T. White, Jacqueline A. Walcott-McQuigg, Claudia J. Gollop, Elizabeth A. Peterson, Diane D. Turner, Patricia Green-Powell, Kim Marie Vaz, and Leslie Ann Kingman.

Yow, Valerie Raleigh. *Recording Oral History: A Practical Guide for Social Scientists.* Thousand Oaks, Calif.: Sage Publications, 1994. This book is a guide for social scientists on oral history methodology and use.

Project Support Sources

Kammen, Carol. *On Doing Local History: Reflections on What Historians Do, Why, and What It Means.* Walnut Creek, Calif.: AltaMira Press, 1986. This book is especially helpful in understanding the importance of local history and how issues of local interest can and do fit into events on regional and national levels.

Kammen, Carol, and Norma Prendergast. *Encyclopedia of Local History,* 15th ed. Walnut Creek, Calif.: AltaMira Press, 2000. This useful volume contains an encyclopedia of useful terms for local historians and four appendices: a list of ethnic group historical organizations, a list of religious group historical organizations, a list of state historical organizations, and a list of National Archives and Records Administration facilities throughout the country. Listings include addresses, telephone numbers, and e-mail contacts.

Kyvig, David, and Myron Marty. *Nearby History,* 2d ed. Walnut Creek, Calif.: AltaMira Press, 2000. This book and its companion volumes are guides to doing local history research. The second edition describes methods for collecting information from a variety of sources, ranging from standard archival collections to the World Wide Web. The "Notes and Further Reading" following the discussion of interviewing contains a list of useful readings. The companion volumes, also available through AltaMira Press, focus on local schools (by Ronald Butchart), houses and homes (by Barbara Howe, Dolores Fleming, Emory Kemp, and Ruth Ann Overbeck), public places (by Gerald A. Danzer), places of worship (by James Wind), and local businesses (by Austin Kerr, Amos J. Loveday, and Mansel G. Blackford).

Rosenzweig, Roy, and David Thelen. *The Presence of the Past: Popular Uses of History in American Life.* New York: Columbia University Press, 1998. In this book, Rosenzweig and Thelen present information collected from 1,500 Americans about their connections to the past and describe how these connections influence their daily lives and their thoughts about the future. Discussions about the place of oral history provide insight into thinking about this field and its opportunities.

American Association for State and Local History (AASLH)

The American Association for State and Local History (AASLH) has a technical leaflet series designed to provide people associated with museums and historical organizations up-to-date information. Technical leaflets are available through the AASLH *History News* magazine or to any interested buyer. Recent technical leaflets on oral history include:

Technical Leaflet #191, "Using Oral History in Museums," by Barbara Allen Bogart. Included in *History News*, volume 50, number 4, Autumn 1995.

Technical Leaflet #210, "A Guide to Oral History Interviews," by Barbara W. Sommer and Mary Kay Quinlan. Included in *History News*, volume 55, number 3, Summer 2000.

Its book series, published by AltaMira Press in California, includes local history, museum management, preservation and conservation, education and interpretation, oral history, material culture, and cultural resource management titles.

Oral History Association (OHA)

In addition to the *Evaluation Guidelines* included in appendix 7, the Oral History Association has pamphlets on specific topics of interest to oral historians. These are:

Oral History and the Law, 3d ed. John Neuenschwander. 2002. The definitive document on oral history legal issues.

Oral History in Community History Projects. Laurie Mercier and Madeline Buckendorf. 1992. A good description of how to use oral history in the community.

Oral History Projects in Your Classroom. Linda Wood. 2001. Written for classroom teachers, it includes sample forms, handouts, curriculum suggestions, and discussion questions.

Oral History Review. Published biannually by the Oral History Association, it includes essays, and book and media reviews relating to the collection, use, and interpretation of oral history.

Index

About the Authors

Mary Kay Quinlan, Ph.D., freelance journalist and oral historian, is editor of the Oral History Association *Newsletter* and has been active in regional and national oral history activities for many years. She was a Washington correspondent for the Omaha *World-Herald* and Gannett News Service for fifteen years and has taught graduate and undergraduate journalism courses at the University of Maryland and the University of Nebraska-Lincoln. She is past president of the National Press Club and is a member of the Gridiron Club of Washington, D.C. Quinlan has conducted oral history workshops, presented at regional and national conferences, and has been a National Endowment for the Humanities peer reviewer for oral history project proposals. She is listed on the Nebraska Humanities Council Humanities Resource Center Speakers' Bureau as an oral history resource. Quinlan holds a B.A. with high distinction from the University of Nebraska-Lincoln, an M.A. in journalism from the University of Maryland, and a Ph.D. in American Studies from the University of Maryland. She currently resides in Lincoln, Nebraska.

Barbara W. Sommer has spent her career in the field of public history. She helped develop a regional archives in Minnesota and for eight years was director of a historical organization that won state and national recognition for its work. She has been an oral historian for more than twenty-five years, serving as director or codirector for numerous oral history projects. Sommer has led oral history workshops, made presentations at state and national conferences, and is a founder of the Oral History Association of Minnesota. She served as a reviewer for the Bush Foundation on its first Native American oral history proposal. Sommer was appointed by the president of the Oral History Association to serve as liaison to the American Association for State and Local History and served on the AASLH *PATHWAYS* project. She is listed on the Nebraska Humanities Council Humanities Resource Center Speakers' Bureau as an oral history resource. She is the owner of BWS Associates, an oral history consulting firm. Sommer holds a B.A. from Carleton College, Northfield, Minnesota, and an M.A. from the University of Minnesota. She currently resides in Lincoln, Nebraska.